D1446855

To Ernestine,
with all best wishes!
Susan Mayall

ALL THE PENNIES IN THE WORLD

An English Wartime Childhood

SUSAN HAYTER MAYALL

WingSpan Press

Copyright © 2017 by Susan Hayter Mayall

All rights reserved.

No part of this book may be reproduced or transmitted in any
form or by any means, electronic or mechanical, including
photocopying, recording or by any information storage and
retrieval system, without written permission from the author,
except for the inclusion of brief quotations in review.

Published in the United States and the United Kingdom
by WingSpan Press, Livermore, CA

The WingSpan name, logo and colophon are the trademarks of
WingSpan Publishing.

ISBN 978-1-59594-608-9 (pbk.)
ISBN 978-1-59594-663-8 (hardcover)

First edition 2017

Printed in the United States of America

www.wingspanpress.com

Library of Congress Control Number: 2017942701

1 2 3 4 5 6 7 8 9 10

TABLE OF CONTENTS

Acknowledgment

My thanks for help and encouragement in writing this memoir to my dear husband Brian. And to my brothers, who put up with so much from me, and still do! Also to all those who read it in its various stages — friends, acquaintances whom I barely knew but hoped would be unbiased - all those good critics who propelled me to continue the endeavor.

And in memory of my parents, who loved each other and us so much, and were separated forever by the madness of war.

Mother, with Howard, Richard and me -1937.

ALL THE PENNIES IN THE WORLD

MY PLACES

Beginnings

I was an English child of the 30s, born in the year Hitler came to power in Germany.

It was a strange time in Britain. So many of the men who would have been husbands and fathers had died in World War I. So many women had been left without partners or children, yet society still didn't allow them many other meaningful roles. Homeless war veterans walked the main Portsmouth London road, searching for work, or asking for food or a drink of water. And the dread of another war hung over everything. Later on, when I read the novels and memoirs of the inter war period I disliked them — they seemed full of darkness. I was surprised to have lived through that time. But in my early childhood I was mostly unaware of any of that.

Sounds, smells, wind and sun, — the rustle of leaves as I lay in my pram for a nap, the comfort of a certain red wool cardigan when I put my arm over my nose and sniffed it, the cream colored canopy overhead and the wind ruffling its silk fringe — these are some of my earliest memories. They were certainly mine, unlike the often repeated story of my remark when told that the great gray ship lying in the harbor below us was the famous battle cruiser Hood. We were high on the Rock of Gibraltar. "I know — I can smell it." I said — and I still think I said it. I can see that ship, and I well remember the odor of paint, warm metal and institutional food in all naval vessels. Do I really remember that day, when I was under three? Who knows? I may be imagining it. But nobody else could remember the view from my pram.

I remember the Dutch ship that took us to Gibraltar to visit our father, who was on the Hood then, and the chocolate sprinkles on our bread at breakfast. And my father meeting us and taking us to shore in a small boat, and giving me a little plastic brooch with three birds sitting on a branch, which I still have. And the Alameda Gardens in Gib,

1

(as it was referred to in Naval/Marine circles), where a boy was flying a kite. There was pain, when I fell and hurt my arm and was taken to the doctor in a little wagon with a white canvas cover, pulled by a small black pony.

Later, during a spell when we lived with our Masson grandparents, there was a doll called "Awful Sight," whom I loved. Her face, with some sort of varnished surface, was scorched — she had once been left too close to the fire. Her name had been bestowed by my grandmother, who never wanted me to take her on walks, and thus be seen in public. And I remember a beautiful muslin dress with blue embroidered spots on it that my aunt Georgie gave me. When I tried it on and pranced down the stairs in it my mother and Georgie laughed so hard at my vanity that I never wanted to wear it again.

And the wonderful smell of hay in the early summer, and the syringa flowers outside our kitchen window, and the lovely hot, sweet smell of ironing clothes that had hung on the line — the taste of fresh green peas, and raspberries from my grandmother's garden. I can hear the call of the rag and bone man as he passed with his worn out old horse — "Ragaboa, ragaboa" or so it sounded to me. And why did he want bones, I wondered? But nobody ever told me. The Italian ice cream man's bell on the little cart he pushed was a special sound, even if we were not allowed to have his ice cream.

The call of the cuckoo meant spring — a bad bird, we were told, because it pushed other fledglings out of the nest. I feel my bare feet in squishy mud as we made mud pies, I feel an earth worm placed in my hand by my father one day, and a time at the beach when I got lost and could see nothing but legs all around me. So much of childhood is simply feeling, sensing, noticing, wondering why.

My Grandmother Masson told us "Never bring May", which is flowering hawthorn, "into the house — it's unlucky!" The same applied to allowing an unfurled umbrella indoors, and to the color green. Why? She could not tell us.

If you're lucky you have people around you who will answer your questions. My grandfathers — both of them — listened and answered seriously. My grandmother Hayter tried. But they weren't there very often. My father always listened and answered, but he was nearly always away on a ship. The problem was that the people we spent most time with — our mother, aunts, my grandma Masson, didn't even attempt to answer any question they found difficult. They laughed, finding us quaint and amusing — or embarrassing — for wanting to know so much.

"Where do babies come from?" I ask. They glance at each other warily. "Under the gooseberry bush!" my mother says. Which even then seemed unlikely. So I grew out of the habit of asking questions. But I watched and I wondered.

When I was small we lived in a series of rented flats and houses, and sometimes, when my father was away, with my mother's parents. My parents never owned a house together By the time I was three and a half we had moved into the house we children all remember as home, the one called 'Rosyth' on the busy London Road in the village of Purbrook, about five miles out of Portsmouth.

We had two big bedrooms, a room we called the nursery, an attic, one bathroom, a kitchen, a dining room and a 'drawing room'. In front was a small lawn, and behind the house a little orchard, a big wooden shed, and a walnut tree with a tall swing hung from one of its branches.

We had no washing machine, no dryer, no mixer, no toaster, no vacuum cleaner, no dishwasher — not even a mechanical egg beater, and no refrigerator. We did have a radio, a telephone, a gas stove, an electric iron, a pantry, and a wind up 'gramophone'.

We had no car — except for a brief period when my father bought one on impulse on his way home on leave and was soundly reprimanded for it by my mother. We saw him driving by while we were on our afternoon walk. And what I remember most about that episode was the mingled joy and annoyance in my mother's voice! I don't even remember if we drove home in it!

What we did have was two parents who were very much in love. They were funny and adventurous, and they loved us too. We had two sets of grandparents, numerous uncles and aunts, cousins, all our mother's friends and their children, and the people who came to our house to deliver groceries or scrubbed the floors or washed the windows. They were all our friends — we took it for granted that to them we were special people.

And we children had each other. That was me, Howard, and Richard, until November 1940, when our sister Sarah was born. We were each other's best friends and companions, rarely, if ever, apart.

I doubt if my mother ever really missed having a toaster, or even a washing machine, though she washed our clothes by hand every single day, and ironed too. We did have toast, of course, even without a toaster — it was made under the grill in the gas oven. But she was suspicious of mechanical objects — could never quite believe that a vacuum cleaner could do as good a job as a stiff brush on a carpet, or a broom on a kitchen floor. And in the thirties and forties not everyone in England had a refrigerator. Her parents had never had one, though her in laws did.

We were happy then, all of us, I think. Until the war came, and that changed nearly everything.

People

We adored our father, though he was rarely home. He was an officer in the Royal Marines, and was always being posted to ships that were sent to faraway places. But when he was home we had his full attention, and he was one of those unusual people who could play with children as an equal. So of course he had an advantage over our mother, who was there all the time and had too much to do to spend her time playing with us.

But she was the one who was largely responsible for our happiness.

I was her first child, born when she had been married nearly two years. When I was very small she used to sing to me as she put me to bed. That was in the earliest days, when Howard and I were both very young. I don't remember a time before Howard, since I was only eighteen months old when he was born. But perhaps I do have a subconscious memory of some of the songs from that earlier time. They were lullabies, sung in her sweet, high soprano, very gently and quietly.

"Go to sleep, my baby,
Close your pretty eyes,
Lulla, lulla baby,
Lulla, lullabye."

The 'Lulla' was always pronounced 'Loola'.

She was soft, silky feeling. She smelt of Vinolia soap, Johnson's baby powder, Coty 'L'Aimant' perfume. Not that I knew the names, but she remained faithful to those products all her life, so I learned them later. Her hair was cobweb fine, and the lightest brown. I liked to run my fingers through it. My father, when he was home, would sing to her the old song "I love my Jeannie with the light brown hair". But her name, we discovered later, was spelt Gene, short for Eugenie — a very big name for someone so tiny. She was five feet tall, small boned, very

5

slim. My father often called her Jennie, which really suited her better.

I grew up to rhymes and games — this one played on bare toes, one at a time.

"This little pig went to market
This little pig stayed at home — "

Another game went with a finger circling the palms of my hands.

"Round and round the garden
Like a teddy bear
One step, two step
Tickly under there!"

And a scarier clapping rhyme.

"My mother said
I never should
Play with the gypsies in the wood.
If I did
She would say,
Naughty girl to disobey."

It ended with a flurry of 'disobeys' and clapping.

There really were gypsies around — they camped in their colorful caravans on grassy patches at the sides of the roads near us, or in the corner of the field opposite. They had barking dogs and dark haired children and clothes lines strung from trees. "Why were the gypsies bad?" I'd ask, but she never told me. It was just a rhyme, she said.

Sometimes she'd sing old music hall songs learnt from her father, some of them quite risqué, and all of them funny, like the one about a man who went to a barber in Brighton "Who shaved off my whiskers and part of my chin". And sometimes it would be cautionary ditties featuring naughty little boys who disobeyed their parents and came to sad ends — "And the verdict was — a pair of skates, broken ice, heaven's gates!" sung with great drama. Other times it was Puck's song from "Midsummer Night's Dream" or "Overhead the moon is beaming" from "The Student Prince" which she'd seen with my father before I was born. And 'Alice Blue Gown' which she loved, and which I can still sing all the way through, though I could never sing as well as she did.

She read to me every night — fairy tales, Beatrix Potter, in the beautiful little original editions, A.A. Milne and "Winnie the Pooh", and all the A.A. Milne rhymes.

My favorite stories were Potter's "Jemima Puddleduck" and "Mrs. Tiggywinkle". I came to know them by heart, and longed to visit the Lake District landscape in the illustrations.

After the songs and rhymes and stories came the goodnight kiss, and often her words "I love you more than all the pennies in the world" which I would sleepily repeat after her.

My brother Howard was born eighteen months after me — at home, before the doctor arrived. He weighed over 10 pounds. Luckily my mother, though tiny herself, was apparently fine after this, and always said she had babies easily.

I can't say I remember this great event. But I think Howard may have missed out on the lullabyes, because I was growing up, and ready for the rhymes and stories. Soon we went on to stories about our mother's own life and family. She told of the time when her older sisters raided their mother's vegetable garden and ate all the new young carrots, sticking their leaves back into the soil. Auntie Gwen had once peed on her own little garden to make it grow better. It was during the First World War, and they were hungry.

She told us about dances on board ships, and camping with our father in Scotland (which she did not enjoy, understandably, since a nest of earwigs fell on her head their first night in a tent.) and about their wedding. This was our favorite story, and we asked for it again and again. We could almost feel the velvet of her ivory colored gown, see the arch of swords created by our father's fellow Royal Marine Officers, and the beautiful lakes at Glendalough in Ireland where they spent their honeymoon.

In those early days she turned duties into games. When she washed my hair, always with Amami shampoo, which came in a paper packet and had to be mixed with warm water, we'd pretend she was a hair stylist and I was her customer. "Well, Modom" — (the pronunciation often used by those who were trying to talk 'proper') — she'd say, as she twirled my foamy hair between her fingers "How would you like to be styled today?" Then I'd have to decide whether to have it curly or piled on top of my head, and she'd bring me a mirror and show me her creation. Sometimes I'd go with her to her own hair appointments, and she'd ask the hair dresser to curl my hair just a little with the hot tongs, making that singeing smell that will always remind me of her.

When Richard was born, two years after Howard, I was jealous for the first time. Our father was home for the birth, the only one of us he was there for, and Howard and I were sent off to our grandparents with a new silver threepenny bit apiece. Our grandfather took us down to Woodcocks, the sweet shop nearby, that he always called "Timberdoodles", and I bought a lollypop with mine. And I remember that lollypop, the thrill of buying it myself, more than I remember my first sight of Richard. For a time I didn't have to notice him, but then I became aware that my mother no longer had as much time for us, especially me. That jealousy didn't last long; Richard became a charming little boy, who loved exploring and adventure and did almost everything I told him to — unlike Howard, who often rebelled at my domineering ways.

My mother did what she could to see that I sometimes had time alone with her. On Friday evenings I'd be allowed to get up after we'd all been put to bed, being careful not to waken my brothers, and I'd spend an hour or so with her on my own. Later Howard was allowed to join me, which wasn't quite the same. But she was always anxious that we should not be jealous of each other — something that had happened in her family, though not so much with her, since she was the favored daughter.

She didn't join in our games, — in fact I remember mornings as always being times when we were left to our own devices, either in our nursery or much more often outside in the garden. But she included us in the things that she enjoyed — we went for walks in the fields and woods opposite our house every afternoon, we went haymaking on our milkman's farm, we went to see traveling circuses and on rides at local fairs.

Sometimes we had tea with Marine wives, also alone while their husbands were overseas. Mostly these families seemed boring compared with ours — the children had playrooms with carpets you had to be careful not to spill anything on, and nannies who made them say grace before meals, and they weren't allowed to climb trees or make mud pies, as we were.

Some friends were old but definitely not boring, like the retired

8

Admiral and his wife who lived in a house with a huge garden, where we were allowed to explore all we liked, and then have wonderful creamy cakes. Or the two old sisters who lived in a flat at the top of an elegant Georgian house, and had a collection of fascinating miniature books and ancient mechanical toys — bike riders and horses and tiny old cars. We were allowed to play with these precious objects, and I don't think we ever broke a thing. I don't know how she knew these people, but she had a wide variety of friends and acquaintances, and these included the people who worked for us, like our 'charlady' Checkers, who lived in a little house in our village.

This was our favorite stop. 'Checkers' had a tiny sweet shop out front, which her son managed, and a toilet in the back yard, which seemed very exotic. We tried to use it every time. She always gave us tea and cookies, and as we left she'd press a penny or two into our palms. We loved her, though we often tormented her as she scrubbed our floors on hands and knees, by snatching her habitual black beret off her head and throwing it behind the sofa. Even when we were teenagers, and came back from Devon to visit, we could never leave her house without a half crown each that she'd bestowed on us. And our milkman, Mr. Plair, invited us out to his farm each year to 'help' with the haymaking, and once even to see a 'Guy Fawkes' burnt on a huge bonfire, and fireworks, which scared me. We drove in his truck across rough grassy meadows to the great fire, with rabbits scattering each side of us in the headlights.

Our mother loved to take us down to Southsea, the fashionable seaside part of Portsmouth, where there were elegant department stores and restaurants. A great treat was to have tea in the café at Handley's, the main department store. A gypsy band would be playing while we ate toast dripping with butter, kept warm in a heavy silver dish with a lid. There would be chocolate éclairs and other exciting delicacies, and a handsome waiter in formal clothes hovering over us, waiting to act on any wish of my mother's. It seemed as if she only had to lift an eyebrow for him to leap into action — but we took it for granted that everyone wanted to please my mother. Not that she was demanding — she just liked people, and immediately talked with them, and they responded. Of course, what we didn't realize, being her children, was how pretty she was, which immediately attracted anyone she came in touch with. And then there was Kimballs, a fancy café that had tea dances, and where our parents once left us up at our table on the balcony while they whirled around the dance floor together.

But elegant tea parties weren't the only thing she gave us a taste for. She loved celery, radishes, raw carrots, anything crunchy — also Brazil nuts that she always wanted us to crack for her because they were so difficult to get into. And sometimes after lunch, our main meal of the day, she'd ask us to fetch the blue and white Chinese jar that sat on the sideboard in our tiny dining room. Then she'd dip a fork into it and pluck a piece of stem ginger dripping with syrup which she popped cleanly into her mouth. Anything ginger was good — ginger snaps, ginger beer, chocolate covered ginger — and the hotter the better. She liked to tell us how she'd once choked on a piece of ginger when someone made her laugh — which she did often and wholeheartedly. "Almost the end of me!" she'd say.

She liked to have us do small things for her — like giving her segments from an orange we'd peeled for ourselves. Perhaps it was because she spent so much time looking after us and other people, like my aunt Georgie, who arrived periodically from her nursing job in London whenever she needed a vacation. And no homeless veteran who came to the door asking for work ever left without a sandwich. She remembered everyone who was sick and visited them, she bought a winter coat for her mother when she didn't have much for herself.

When my mother was tired — which she rarely showed — she would ask us to brush her hair. She loved the slow sweep of the coarse bristles against her scalp, especially when one brushed it upwards from her neck. Nobody seemed to look after my mother. My father was always getting posted to ships overseas, and even when he came back he wanted a bit of looking after himself.

Even if he actually made more work for her, things were different when he was home. There was a sparkle about those days — because my parents were still madly in love. They kissed, held hands, danced in our little 'drawing room', and did not allow us into their big bed at night. Each time he came home, seldom for long, was another honeymoon. And we did exciting things that we didn't do otherwise — we went on expeditions by bus to strange places, had picnics on hill tops and visited ruined castles. We sailed the model Chinese junks he'd brought back from China for us.

The only hints of disharmony we ever had was when my mother was desperate to go out with him — desperate to have a break in the monotony of life with three small children and very little money or help. He was happy simply being home — while she must have longed to have him on her own and feel young and carefree again. I don't think they ever went out together without us until his very last posting, when he was mostly living at home. I think they had very little money — he was just a Captain — and they certainly couldn't afford regular help with us. But he did very often take us out on our own. Perhaps that was a relief for her, but I wonder if she really wanted to be left alone again.

She had friends, she had family, and everyone we met seemed to love her. Her parents lived only a mile away. She was very close to two of her sisters. They, and her oldest friend whom she'd known since she was six, visited us regularly. But most of the time the person she needed most was not there. Perhaps her stories about her earlier years of marriage were a way of reliving them — times when she and my father were together more of the time.

Sometimes after I'd gone to bed I'd tiptoe downstairs, as I used to do when I thought I heard burglars breaking in, or simply wanted to make sure she was there. I remember how silent the house used to be. Although we had an old wind up gramophone and a radio these were never on. Perhaps she needed peace after a day with us, or was afraid of waking us up. I'd stand quietly on the stairs watching her, as she ironed, or 'aired' damp washing in front of the gas fire, or just sat reading or knitting in the rocking chair. She often didn't notice as I stood there, and jumped when I made some sound. Then I'd be allowed to sit with her for awhile, before she took me up to bed again — my own bed, never hers. At night her bed was reserved for herself and my father, even when he wasn't home.

All we knew about her was what she told us, which wasn't much, and was never about her feelings or desires — and what we observed for ourselves. We were completely dependent on her — she was the authority, she governed our lives. The power was lightly held. We didn't resent it; within her framework we felt secure, protected, and almost free.

Walks

R egular meals, daily baths, early bedtimes — these were all part of what English middle class parents of the thirties believed their children needed.

My mother, in many ways a rebel against accepted wisdom, also believed in all these. Our routine included fresh air and exercise, both of which she enjoyed herself. She had been an enthusiastic tennis player before we were born, loved the countryside, and walked everywhere, as did all her family.

So at some point, on virtually every day of our childhood, we would be dragged away from whatever we were doing and taken for a walk. We never wanted to go. It was much more fun digging holes in the garden for underground forts, or making mud pies to bake in an 'oven' formed from a discarded pram, or passing caterpillars through my 'wet-tums' doll. 'Going for a walk' was always interrupting something fun.

What made it worse was that we had to get cleaned up and changed into fresh clothes, into garments my mother considered appropriate for us to be seen in by outside observers. So, morning or afternoon — and more often it was afternoon, — we were stripped to the skin, scrubbed down from head to foot, and dressed in clean, ironed clothes, shorts and shirts for the boys, a dress for me, white ankle socks and brown leather shoes for all of us, and wool coats to go over the top. When we were really small we all had identical yellow coats and red shoes, and must have looked adorable.

All this took awhile, with three of us — not to mention baby Sarah when she came along. My Aunt Georgie once suggested that we could just put on our coats over our play clothes. My mother was shocked, and annoyed with Georgie for even thinking of something so slovenly. She took extra care that day to make sure our hair was brushed and our shoes shining bright. I, of course, agreed with Georgie, but would never have dared say so. One did not disagree with my mother.

Warmth or comfort were not real considerations in preparing for these expeditions. Yes, we wore coats if the weather was cool, and we might even be allowed to wear woolly mittens. But our heads and our knees were bare. My mother didn't approve of hats for children, or trousers. I never wore slacks till I was eighteen, and the boys wore shorts till they went to boarding school at age eleven or twelve.

We never questioned all this, and in fact I don't remember feeling cold on these walks. That's because, once we were outside the garden gate, everything changed. Unlike our doctor's children, whom we'd see holding hands with their nanny and walking sedately along the road, we had adventures on our walks. All care for our appearance disappeared as soon as we were away from the house.

"Let's race!" my mother would say, and she'd take off, pushing the high English pram in front of her, slim legs flashing in their silk stockings and high heels, soft brown hair blowing loose in the breeze, while we on our shorter legs puffed along behind her. She always won, of course.

But even on the rare occasions when we walked along the road there were diversions — walls to balance on, puddles to jump, bushes to shake after a rainstorm so that drops fell all over us. There were dogs to pat, and once I even gave one a piece of pastry that I'd rolled on the floor while my mother made a pie. Being somewhat gray it was deemed unsuitable for consumption by humans, but the dog liked it.

Most of the time, though, we didn't keep to the roads. We took off on the muddy footpath across the fields opposite 'our' house, which led across streams, through woods, past farms, over stiles and five barred gates.

I should explain that in England then, and to some degree now, farmland was open to the public wherever there was a public footpath. Even more than that, trespassing could not be prosecuted unless damage was done. The footpaths, most of them dating from the Middle Ages, connected farms, villages, went across fields and through woods and farmyards, sometimes led simply to the top of the highest hill. So we were lucky in having farmland across the street.

If it was really wet we children wore rubber boots, but my mother always wore her elegant high heeled pumps. "I can't walk in low heels" she'd say if anyone commented on this. She loved to walk, but she also loved her slim, beautiful legs, and knew what showed them to best advantage. Not that there was anyone much to look at them there in the muddy fields, apart from an occasional laborer digging up turnips or a cowhand collecting his herd. It was a matter of pride, as it was to dress us like fashion plates each afternoon.

She didn't even talk to us much, as our father did on the rare occasions he was home. She expected us to enjoy the things she did — walking and running, the countryside in all weathers, wildflowers and birds, the smell of celery on a winter's day, wood smoke — or even more peat smoke, which reminded her of her honeymoon in Ireland. "I love that smell!" she'd exclaim, breathing deeply, head thrown back.

In the spring, when primroses began to push up from the dead brown leaves that covered the ground in the woods, we'd pick huge bunches of the fragile yellow flowers, learning to pinch off the thin stems at their bases, and surrounding each bunch with crinkly leaves. The primroses had a damp, honeyish scent, and we filled the house with them. The next month, in May, the woods were filled with bluebells, but my mother never let us pick them. "They don't last" she said "And besides, they don't grow back the way primroses do."

One of our best occasional adventures was when we passed a cowshed where milking was going on. My mother would confidently step inside, careful to avoid the cowpats on the ground. She'd scan the shed for the cowman. In most of these farms the milking was still done by hand, and even in those that had milking machines the cows' udders still had to be 'stripped' by hand. So usually there'd be a cloth capped male, in ancient waistcoat, shirt sleeves rolled up, cigarette hanging from a corner of his mouth, hauling on the pink teats of a placid cow as he sent thin streams of milk hissing into a pail.

My mother loved fresh milk. She would ask for a mug as if it was her right, but always with a smile. Of course, she was never refused. We drank some of it too, all warm, foamy and full of cream. Perhaps that's why I test positive for TB today — I'm sure those cows were not TB tested. But what a difference between the taste of that milk and what we drink now.

We learned to like the things she did, partly because we wanted her to be happy, but in time because we enjoyed them ourselves. And I particularly enjoyed the fact that we were free, once we'd got into the countryside, to explore and devise our own activities. We built dams in creeks, climbed any possible tree, played hide and seek (often with her), played cricket or rounders with sticks for bats and wickets.

But we couldn't supply her with her major need, that of companionship. Our conversation was obviously limited. For that she needed other adults. So sometimes we ended up at the grocery store, where Mr. Wiggs and my mother gossiped while she placed an order to be delivered later, and we children munched cookies handed out from the big square tins that lined the front of the counter.

Other times it might be Wadhams, the draper and outfitter, where old Mr. Wadham would fit us with 'Start Rite' shoes, or Gauntlett's, the dairy, where we might even sit at a table upstairs and have tea and hot buttered toast. All the shopkeepers knew my mother — she had grown up just down the road in Widley, and her face had shown up in most photographers' windows. When a girl she'd been much in demand as a model since she had perfect bone structure.

On many walks my mother collected companions, people she could giggle with over jokes we didn't understand, share news of far off husbands, talk about children and everyday problems. Vonnie Tillard, Maureen Stapleton, Janet Cornelius — all service wives, spending most of their time alone with their children, whom sometimes we liked, more often didn't. The adults strolled along, forgetting us, while we waded through streams or rolled down muddy banks.

How did she manage clean clothes each day, I wonder? The dried mud must have been removed with a stiff bristled brush, the socks and pants and shirts and skirts washed by hand in the sink, and hung on the line outside or draped over a rack in the kitchen. Our shoes would have the dirt scraped off, the polish applied, the leather buffed with a brush and soft cloth. All this was achieved sometime in the gaps between walks — but we never noticed it happening.

We always knew when our Aunt Georgie had arrived for a visit by the wonderful aromas of bathsalts and expensive soaps that filled the house. She was a nurse, and unmarried, though she did have a boyfriend called Uncle Bert. My mother didn't think much of Uncle Bert, but she thought it was high time Georgie got married. Georgie had bunions and sore feet caused by long hours in uncomfortable shoes on hard hospital floors. So she didn't like to walk far, and hated our squishy, muddy tracks across the fields. She was also nervous, and would cry out in terror if one of us jumped off a high gate, or ran too close to traffic. Yet later on she nursed war casualties during the Blitz, so she must have had courage.

She annoyed my mother with her nerves and her dithering. My mother's absolute favorite companion for walks was her friend May Wroe, whom she'd met on her first day of school at the age of six. May was tall, with a pink and white complexion, huge blue eyes and a sweet smile. She too was a nurse, at a big hospital in Kent, and later became its 'matron'.

We adored her; she listened to us without laughing, and talked to us as if we were grown up people. I felt instinctively that I'd much rather have her as a nurse than Georgie, who teased us all the time, and was very bossy. I even wished once, rather guiltily, that May was my mother. We would never be adults to my mother.

But of course Georgie and May were seldom there, because of their jobs, and the other nearby relative, Auntie Iris, had two little boys and a very sick husband. She looked after him all the time, as well as our cousins Peter and Simon, and when he died she had to sell their house, move in with a friend and go to work. She was my favorite aunt, because she always listened to me, even if she never came for walks with us.

There were so many walks with my mother. So it seems unfair that I should remember in vivid detail the walks that we did with my father. I say 'we', but often they were with me alone. When I was very young, probably before he went off to China on the aircraft carrier 'Eagle', we would go across the field as usual, but instead of keeping to the path we'd branch off to where a five barred gate led to a track completely overgrown with tall grasses, vines and brambles. This was 'the tiger path', so christened by my father. It must have reminded him of his own childhood in India, when he and his brothers and sisters would go camping in the jungle with his parents. We would get down on our stomachs and wiggle along under the leaves and branches, listening all the time for a roar or a suspicious rustle in the bushes. I knew there weren't really any tigers there — but all the same!

Another time we sat on a pile of gravel left by workers on a road lined by sweet chestnut trees. We had a tea party — there were actually four of us — I had two imaginary friends at that time, Mrs. Dorby and Mrs. Meety. The chestnut leaves were plates and the gravel made the cakes. "Would you like another cup of tea, my dear?" "Yes please — and another cake too." "Thank you so much, my dear."

There was a walk past a gypsy caravan, when he told me about the gypsies' roving life, and another when he stopped a boy with a huge cart horse, and asked him to give me a ride on the high, swaying back.

To Howard, Richard and me he was the epitome of daring and gallantry. On one of his last visits home, in midwinter England, the three of us walked across the familiar fields opposite our house, Richard clutching his Christmas present, a large wooden clockwork motorboat. Beyond some woods was a large pond, and we set the boat in the murky water, aimed at the opposite bank. Disaster! A thin layer of ice covered the center of the pond, and the boat got stuck in it. Richard's face puckered up in dismay. My father pulled off his shoes and socks, rolled up his trousers and waded out to the stricken vessel. Rescue was achieved, while I, echoing the words my mother might have used, told him he'd catch his death of cold, and maybe we should get him a cup of tea at the nearby farmhouse. But he only laughed, not the sort of laugh that made one feel bad, but a friendly, funny laugh.

And one day, after the bombing started, we walked with him to Purbrook Common, one of the old public spaces where medieval farmers had grazed their herds, and where sheep still cropped the short turf. It was late in the afternoon, and just after rain — the grass was wet, and the soil slippery. There was a small air raid shelter in the center of the common. We explored it; it was flooded, as so many of the shelters were, having been built with more enthusiasm than expertise. After we'd seen the inside we climbed up on the grass covered roof, high enough to be a little scary. But my father was never scared. He jumped from the roof across the entrance, and he did it again and again, while we changed from nervousness to mirth, and I laughed so hard I wet my pants. He carried them back in one hand, holding mine in the other, as we walked home in the dusk past cottage windows with mellow light showing through the chinks in their blackout curtains.

My Father

It's easy to glamorize someone you seldom saw and who disappeared before you were eight years old. I wonder often how my father would have seemed to me if he'd survived the war and I'd known him when I was a teenager, a young woman or a middle aged parent. My memories of him from my early childhood would surely have been less vivid, being overlaid by later experiences and emotions.

He was born in India, the eldest son of a British district commissioner of police. His mother's family had been in India since the 1830s, and in fact her grandmother had been Indian — a fact our generation was the first to discover, much, much later. He had a free and much loved childhood, surrounded by siblings and other relatives. British children were usually sent back to Britain to go to school, and when my father was ten that happened to him too. But he was luckier than many — he had a friendly aunt in Scotland who looked after him and other expatriate cousins while their parents were abroad. He went to a famous Scottish School, Dollar Academy, which was actually co-ed — something very rare in Britain then. He did brilliantly in school. I have old leather bound copies of books he won as prizes for Latin and French, for Geography and History. But he was also captain of the Rugby team, and a ferocious boxer. He hiked and camped in the Scottish Highlands with his cousins. He should have gone to University, but there were four siblings and not much money, so with his love of adventure and talent for languages he joined the Royal Marines.

I know his interests from the books that sat on the shelves of my parents' glass fronted bookcase. There were the novels of Sigrid Undset, the Norwegian writer. There was "Max Havelaar" the classic Dutch novel about the evils of colonialism. There was Hitler's "Mein Kampf", and "Grey Wolf", the biography of Turkey's independence leader Kemal Ataturk — and the travel/adventure books by Peter Fleming.

"The Forsyte Saga", "Anthony Adverse" and "The Good Earth", the best sellers of the thirties, sat next to T.E. Lawrence's "Seven Pillars of Wisdom" and Edward Lear's Nonsense Verses. It was obvious that he was interested in ideas, in politics, in far off places. In time I devoured all these books myself, longing, as he must have done, to go to Tibet after reading Fleming's "News from Tartary", or to Norway to visit the scenes of "Kristin Lavransdatter".

He was 28 and a Lieutenant when he met and married my mother, who was, appropriately, a librarian. He wasn't tall, but was slim and fit, with deep set, dark blue eyes, a high forehead and a balding head. Even at that young age there were deep crinkles at the corners of his eyes when he laughed — and he laughed a lot. But he was quiet and somewhat shy, which must have appealed to her. She was lively enough herself. Quiet people always attracted her.

I presume the marines decided to train him as an interpreter when they discovered he already spoke several languages. I was conceived in Holland where he was taking a course in Dutch. Photos show my parents clowning together in a suburban garden, flower pots on their heads, or laughing as my mother tried smoking his pipe. Our various homes were later filled with prints of Dutch interiors, and little brass ornaments they'd picked up in sidewalk markets. It was probably the last time they'd have alone together, and ever after my mother talked about Holland nostalgically.

By the time I was born in 1933 he was away in a ship off Trieste in the Mediterranean. Officers didn't get leave to see newborn babies in those days, but when the telegram arrived he took an overnight train across Europe and arrived unannounced in my mother's hospital room. He saw me, reassured himself that I and my mother were doing well, then went straight back — two nights and two days of non-stop travel, some of it in an enclosed compartment with no access to a toilet. He had to pee out of a window — or so I've been told! Unauthorized adventures like this were not good for his career — but it seems that other things were often more important to him.

I, of course, have no consciousness of those early days. But there are sensations, scents that remind me of him — the rasp of rough tweed against my cheek, the warmth of an arm round my shoulders, the aroma of pipe tobacco and 4711 cologne. And I see myself through his eyes in the photos he took of me, a tiny girl in a sun bonnet, dwarfed by tall flowers in a garden — or perched on a high stone wall, a bandana (undoubtedly his) tied jauntily round my head — or the one I love best, myself, wispy haired, held close to his smiling craggy face and gazing trustfully out at the world.

He was away when my brother Howard was born, eighteen months later — home for Richard, two years after that, and away again for Sarah's birth, well into the war years in 1940. After Richard was born we didn't see him for two whole years — he was on the aircraft carrier Eagle patrolling the China seas. Letters would come on flimsy blue air-mail paper, most of them for our mother, but some of them for us. He sent drawings of Chinese dragons and mandarins and junks, and stories of his expeditions to Chinese villages where he tried to learn the language from the peasants. He sent a postcard to Richard, when Richard was much too young to appreciate it. But Howard and I thought it was very funny. On the front was a picture of a swimming duck, with the rhyme "If the sea was beer, and I was a duck, I'd swim to the bottom and never come up." On the back were the words "To little rogue Richard, Lots of love, and hugs and kisses — and kiss Mummy for me, all over." I think it was not really meant for Richard!

At night, we would end our rather perfunctory prayers with "God bless dear Daddy" but we never forgot him anyway.

We children never knew when he'd arrive. Once after a long absence he appeared in the middle of the night when I woke with an upset stomach, throwing up all over the bed. He cleaned me up, gave me warm water to drink (supposed to be easier on the stomach), kissed me and sent me off to sleep again. We knew we were not expected to share our parents' bed when he was home — that was understood — but in the mornings it was different. Then we'd pile into bed with him while my mother bathed and dressed. Under the fuzzy green bedspread we'd pretend to be rabbits in a burrow, or listen to stories of his childhood in India, of cobras in bathtubs and tiger hunts on elephants. And up the stairs would come an odor I associate with his presence, the smell of field mushrooms frying, something we never had when he was not home, because none of us liked them. My mother would cook them for his breakfast as a special treat.

They would snuggle together on the sofa in the evenings, and if they ever went out together they went arm in arm, or hand in hand. We teased them, called them 'soppy', hid our eyes if they kissed. I wonder if we would remember them so clearly, young and in love, if we'd known them tired and middle aged, irritated perhaps with each other. Did they make us idealize marriage, set our standards unrealistically high?.

On rainy days we might go to my grandparents for tea, and once inside their gate my father and I would head for the little holly trees on each side of their front door. We'd crouch under one of them, and my father would shake the trunk until drips fell all over us, and my grandmother would exclaim "You'll catch your death of cold!" — but we never did. He took me to ruined castles, where we climbed crumbling steps to turrets looking out on the misty countryside. We found a dolmen, a Neolithic tomb, and he told me about the long ago people who built it. We went together to buy a book about birds when I wanted to identify them. And he made me climb the terrifying swaying steps to the top of a double decker bus, and waited while I jumped off high banks into his arms. I was not intended to be a frail, fearful girl. His mother had hunted tigers in India and shot game for their meals on camping expeditions. I think it would not have occurred to him that my life should be limited because I was female. And when I hike or travel alone today, I realize that my enjoyment must be partly due to that early conditioning.

Nearly all the children we knew had fathers who were Marine officers. It seemed normal to us that our father should seldom be home. Our grandfathers were both retired; my mother's brothers had 'nine to five' jobs, but we didn't see much of them. One of them, in fact, never came home during the time we lived in Purbrook. He was an accountant in Shanghai, and was interned by the Japanese during the war. So we weren't familiar with fathers who led normal lives. And my mother encouraged us to think that being in the Marines was much better than any other job — other jobs were boring, she said. I think she meant that men who did them were boring too! I certainly grew up thinking I had to marry a soldier or sailor — the only question was 'Which?' And in fact when my father was wearing his 'dress blues', with a red stripe down the trousers, a dazzling white belt and a white helmet, he certainly looked more glamorous than any other man. But occasionally we saw the effect that his prolonged absences had on my mother.

I do remember vividly one particular day. My father was home on leave. It was a wet, gray day, the rain pouring down outside as we sat in the drawing room after lunch. My father, in an armchair near the window, was gradually dropping off to sleep and jerking awake every now and then. Richard, who must have been nearly three at the time, was playing on the floor. He found his way to my father and climbed up the chair and onto his lap. My father, half asleep, slapped him as one might have swatted a fly. Richard's mouth opened and he let out a howl of shock.

I don't know what was said, but in a moment or two, it seemed, we were bundled up in raincoats and boots and hustled out of the door. My mother marched us without a word along the drenched streets, through puddles and mud. There was no play on this day — Howard and I followed in silent misery. I had no understanding for my mother, no sympathy for Richard, but lots for my father.

In time her pace slowed, she turned the pram around, and we went back home. My father was waiting in the kitchen. There was a pot of tea, toast and cake on the table, the first and only time I'd ever seen him do anything in the kitchen. This must have led to reconciliation. My parents snuggled together on the sofa, the three of us played by the fire. All was well in our world after all.

When we went into Southsea on the top of the bus we'd look down on first the Army Barracks, then the Naval ones, until finally we came to Eastney, the glorious eighteenth century Marine Barracks, all glowing red brick and green lawns. We'd sneer at the inferior homes of the Army and Navy, and tell each other how much better Eastney was. We'd sometimes go there to see a Sunday Church Parade, with my father in his dress uniform marching along to the stirring sounds of the famous Marine band. It was led by one of the men who had been at his wedding, Vivian Dunn, later knighted by King George VI.

We were proud of our father — we were proud of the Marines. He and they added color and glamour to our lives. But mostly we simply loved him.

My Mother and Her Family

There was never any doubt in our minds that our parents loved each other deeply. I think they may have met at the library she worked for, or maybe at some Marine party. My mother was much in demand in her twenties, being fun, flirtatious, a great dancer and tennis player, and extremely pretty. Her face was quite well known, because of her part time modeling for a local photographer. She had many suitors, and often showed us bits of jewelry she'd received from them. We even learnt some of their names — I remember one called Donald Brock, a Naval officer who came from Guernsey and gave my mother a beautiful amethyst bracelet. Fortunately it wasn't till after she died that we discovered they were not amethysts after all!

When my father came along she teased him by singing the popular song "Only make believe I love you..." but in fact, of course, she did. When my father asked for her hand in marriage my grandfather said humorously "It's your funeral, old man" because she had been a flighty and strong minded girl, but from then on she was totally loyal — though not above a little mild flirtation with an attractive male!

Her background was completely different from my father's. She had never been out of England, and in fact had never been far from Portsmouth. She'd obviously had a fairly good education at a local girls' school, but had probably left at the age of sixteen. She was a great reader, however, and was always well up on what was going on in the world — and she loved music of all sorts, theater and ballet, and had excellent taste in art and decoration. She dressed elegantly even though she was never well off. And she was fun — she loved circuses and country fairs and roller coasters and parties.

She was, I think, much more fun than the rest of her family, who tended to take themselves more seriously.

She was the sixth of seven children, Fred, Gwen, Iris, Georgina,

Stanley, and Billy. And she was not only her parents' favorite, but her siblings' also. She was the one who got on with all of them, though that didn't mean she liked them all equally. Fred was a lot older than her, and had probably left for Shanghai when she was a young teenager. Gwen was married to Guy Ede, who sold prosthetic devices. She was a petty snob, very concerned about what the neighbors in her suburban Surrey village thought of her. She hung her laundry on her back porch so that they wouldn't see it, to our amusement. Their two children were our oldest cousins, Elspeth and Basil.

Iris was our favorite aunt. She and her husband Rob had two boys, Peter and Simon. Rob was a high school principal, and was already ill with cancer by the time I got to know him. But he was one of the rare relatives that my mother totally approved of. He died just before the war. It was before the National Health Service in England, which would have paid all his medical costs, and they had spent all their savings on his treatment. Iris and the boys had to leave their pleasant little house and move into rooms belonging to a spinster friend of Iris'. The boys went to boarding school on scholarships, while Iris got a job in a bank. Peter was 9, Simon 5. Those two boys were our best friends, and I had a crush on Peter, my big cousin who could already ride a bike. I can still feel the joy of a wobbly ride on the carrier seat, clutching Peter.

Although Iris and my mother were probably the brightest of the siblings and always got on well together, our grandmother could not stand Iris. We heard that Grandma once flung a plate of peas at her during a family dinner, and didn't see her for months on end, even though they lived on the same street. And when we went to visit our grandparents later on we always had to say our goodbyes and make sure Grandma thought we were gone before going on to visit Aunt Iris just up the road. Otherwise we too might be ostracized!

Georgie I've mentioned before. Pretty, sweet, kind and generous, she spoilt it all by being so nervous and having so little self confidence that she was never quite at ease. Luckily, she had escaped her formidable mother who preferred that none of her daughters had jobs. An older family friend whom, much later, she married, helped her to apply to nursing school. And in her nursing career she seems to have been a different, and successful, person. We loved her, but made fun of her — as did our mother.

24

We scarcely knew Uncle Stanley, but we liked him, his wife, Ivy, and their two boys. And Uncle Billy seems to have been the black sheep of the family — there was some sort of cloud over his head which we could feel but never understood. We didn't like him when we saw him, which was seldom. Perhaps his problem was drink, because he was somewhat overweight, with loose, shiny red lips, and a flushed complexion. My grandfather drank a little too much also, I think, though only beer at the local pub., and never in my grandmother's presence. But it never affected our love for him.

There was a time, probably when my mother was expecting Sarah, that Howard, Richard and I went over to our grandparents every Friday. We'd go on the bus by ourselves –a great adventure, since I was only seven, the boys six and four. Always, unless the rain was pelting down, we went for a walk with our grandfather on the Portsdown Hills, just above the streets of pseudo Tudor houses where they lived. We'd go, hand in hand, up through the new houses just being built on the north side of the hill, onto the grassy summit where you could see down over the whole of Portsmouth and its harbor, the Isle of Wight and the forts out at sea. There were forts on the hill too, old red brick buildings partly underground, built in the early nineteenth century to repel Napoleon, who never arrived. Now my grandfather said they were used for growing mushrooms in their cool, dark interiors.

Sometimes the boys stayed with my grandmother, and Grandpa and I would set out with Whisky, the Scotty who used to be ours till my mother found him too much to look after. I had walked one rainy day with my father to pick him up when he was a tiny puppy from the kennels where he was born. Now he rambled about looking for rabbits while my grandfather and I found paths through little glades full of bluebells in the spring, and talked about everything we saw — the new houses, acorns, ships out at sea, an air raid drill with people carrying stretchers. He told me stories too, of skating on frozen ponds when he was young and wearing a coat with a cape around it, and tales of the imaginary doings of "the dog and the horse", all of which I've forgotten. And sometimes my grandmother would pack up a picnic basket full of delicious sandwiches and her home baked cakes and we'd all go off to sit on the grass in a 'dell', as they called it — probably an old quarry overgrown now with trees and vines, where big boys swung from the vines as I watched enviously. My grandmother, unlike my mother, couldn't even see us running down a hill without calling out anxiously "Careful now! You'll fall!" We could never join those boys.

Our grandparents were already retired when we were born. Grandpa had been an engineer, on ships, railways, and in the Naval Docks at Portsmouth. He would often point out the great Naval hammerhead crane he had helped to build. It's still there, part of the Dockyard Museum. He was a small man, with a droopy white moustache, and a nose that was always shiny red. In summer he wore cream tussore silk suits and a Panama hat, in winter a grey flannel suit and a felt trilby. I never saw him in anything informal, and neither he nor my grandmother ever went out without a hat. If he was mowing his immaculate little lawn or trimming his high privet hedge from a step ladder he would remove his jacket and work in his waistcoat and shirt. He never got sweaty, even when he'd walked up and down the Portsdown Hill to do the shopping. He smoked a pipe and had a rather disgusting spittoon by his fireside chair. But we loved him unreservedly, as he loved us. He talked with us, told us stories, explained interesting things, made his version of 'French Toast' — thin white bread buttered then toasted on a long brass fork by the fire. He called me 'Sweet'eart', dropping the H. His knees were bony, but it was warm and comforting to sit on them.

Grandma was a different matter. She was hard to love. Also tiny, with soft white hair and a perfect pink and white complexion that had never seen soap or face cream (so she said), she had a pointy nose that went white when she was annoyed. Our mother told us that, and we were careful to watch out for it. She was annoyed often, though not with us — mostly with our grandfather, who was always doing things wrong, or with Auntie Iris. But my mother, before she was married, had shocked her puritanical mother, who discovered her upstairs wearing only a slip while my father waited downstairs for her to change for a party. My grandmother assumed the worst, to my mother's indignation. We didn't quite understand the implications of this story when she told us, but it must have made quite an impact on my mother, because she repeated it many times.

Grandma didn't like most of her neighbors, and wouldn't speak to them. She was a brilliant cook, and her cakes and cookies were delicious, but she hugged us too hard, and scrubbed our arms and legs before we went home to get rid of the dirt we'd acquired on our walks with Grandpa. We always left with uncomfortable damp legs. Her great joy was her roses, which flourished around their tiny pseudo Tudor house — she kept track of the number she picked each year, and told us the rising numbers with pride.

I should have liked her more, because she undoubtedly loved me and was always good to us all, but there was something forbidding about her dislike of other people, especially Aunt Iris, Peter and Simon. This characteristic of Grandma's affected the whole family, made them jealous and suspicious of each other. Even my mother suffered from it to some degree, mistrusting anyone who seemed to be over important or too much of a 'do gooder'. But my mother loved her parents, and teased them in a way that none of the other siblings seemed able to do. She never got into trouble, like poor Aunt Iris.

I think our mother had broken away in her own fashion, without hurting their feelings or really offending them. Her views on sex, religion, respectability in general, were not far from those of her parents. In other words, these were things you didn't talk about — you just kept to the rules. You didn't go to church, but were shocked by atheism. You flirted, went out with lots of men, but still believed that sex should wait for marriage. You dressed appropriately for the occasion — but could forget it all and climb on a motor cycle in a sundress and high heels if you felt like it.

Our grandparents loved my father, but were probably uncomfortable with his parents, whose lives had been so different from theirs. Luckily they rarely, if ever, met after our parents' wedding.

These grandparents were Victorians, settled in their ways and their beliefs. In their house nothing ever changed — the brass paperweight on the desk, shaped like a lady's high boot — the ancient gramophone with a large horn that stood in the corner by the fireplace, the framed photos of George V and Edward VIII, the blue and white Willow Pattern plates arrayed along the picture rail that ran around the living room — they all belonged to an earlier era. As did they. Grandpa kept up with the news, and listened to the radio, but most of Grandma's conversation was about the past, and she told the same stories again and again.

The Hayters

My father's family, the Hayters, were less familiar and much more interesting. My mother was fascinated by them and wary of them. I don't remember any stories about my Hayter grandparents, but from the tone of her voice when she talked about them I guessed that she wasn't comfortable with them. The clothes Grandma Hayter sent us were never 'in good taste' — they were too frilly, or the fabric was too flashy, or the style was too adult. Of course I usually loved those clothes, but didn't dare say so.

These grandparents lived next to the Crystal Palace, that enormous glasshouse built for the Great Exhibition of 1851. It had been moved from Hyde Park after the exhibition, and re erected in a park in Sydenham. It was tall enough to hold the reconstructed trunk of a Giant Sequoia from Calaveras County in California — we pass its home every time we go up to our cabin in the Sierra Nevada. You can still see its sad, stripped trunk towering above the other trees. And when I see it I never fail to remember the times I was taken to visit the duck pond in front to the Palace, and the photos in the newspaper showing the charred remains of the Glass Castle, as I called it, when it burned to the ground in 1936.

There's a painting by Pissarro of an avenue in Sydenham, a London suburb, which must have been the one our grandparents lived on, or one just like it. The avenue is lined with tall red brick Edwardian houses, set back from the road, surrounded by trees and shrubs. I believe they settled there when my grandfather retired and came back from India. He was still in his forties. At least one of his five children was still at school — Francis, the youngest. He was sent to Dulwich College, very close by. I have wondered how they were able to buy this house — I can't believe Grandpa's income can have been huge. But he came from an old and prosperous family, who had been sheep farmers and

28

wool merchants in Winterbourne Stoke, near Stonehenge. His father had been a shipping merchant in London. Our grandfather must have had some independent income.

In any case it was the first really big house I remember, and always full of people — our uncles and aunts, cousins, friends back from India and other parts of the Empire — a constant babble of voices. I could feel that our mother felt out of place with all these people who shared so much background — or that now is my interpretation of her discomfort. But I loved it. Lying on the sofa in the drawing room on an occasion when we'd arrived in a 'pea soup' fog, and I'd thrown up in the taxi, I felt surrounded by excitement — people who knew me, even if I didn't know them — people who talked differently, argued, laughed a lot, hugged and kissed each other a lot.

In the midst of it all was my Grandmother, dark eyed, curly haired. Already a little stout, slightly ponderous in her movements, dressed in dark colored, shapeless clothes that my mother wouldn't have touched, she was still the center of the room. People flowed around her, tossing remarks at her, which she answered in a low, rather singsong voice. There was no doubt who controlled the household — it was certainly not the one she called 'Tubs', our grandfather. She had been beautiful, and had the confidence that this often gives. Here was a woman who knew her own mind, and wasn't afraid to express it. Doubtless this was another reason my mother was uncomfortable — she mistrusted strong women, being one herself.

Grandma Hayter wasn't afraid to suggest different ways to raise children. She cooked, when she did cook, mostly Indian food, and she was no housewife. I loved the unusual comfort of the rather messy house — and probably showed it. None of this pleased my mother, who had her own very definite ideas about raising children, cooked nothing but plain English food, and kept her house sparkling all the time.

She felt no happier with our father's sisters, Marjorie and Janet. They also had dark eyes and hair, but were quite different from each other. Marjorie was said to be 'delicate' — a description that caused our mother, and therefore us children, to feel some scorn for the person so described. She was lively and 'artistic' — would occasionally get up and demonstrate her flowing modern dance techniques. "Showing off!" my mother would have said, or at least thought. She was married to

Uncle Murray, a gruff Scottish lawyer. They had two children then, timid creatures, we thought, the ages of Howard and Richard. But I don't remember them at Sydenham. Aunt Janet, the opposite of Marjorie, full of vigor, outspoken and opinionated, full of ideas and organization, was equally alien to my mother. She employed German nannies for her two, later three, children — and the idea of nannies, especially German ones, was anathema to my mother. She and her accountant husband lived in Madrid, and only came 'home' rarely.

My father's two younger brothers, though, were a different matter. She loved both of them, and they, like most men, were charmed by her. She told us often how they had both hiked down from London, over sixty miles, to see me when I was born, and had arrived blistered and barefoot but cheerful. And how Uncle Francis had zoomed over our house when he was training in the Royal Air Force, and had dropped a box of chocolates in the garden.

Jimmy was already quite a successful actor on the London stage. He had a glamorous wife, another Marjorie, red headed and friendly. We children loved her — she literally would get down on the floor with us and pretend serious injury or disease so that we could 'treat' her with our pretend medicines. Jimmy was funny — he put on strange faces and voices. He didn't actually play with us, but we found him entertaining and interesting. And Francis was quieter and shyer and looked more like our father. We hardly knew him, but liked him because of his appearance and because he didn't try to make us do things. He must have been very young in the Sydenham years — was probably at Oxford at the time. They adored and looked up to my father.

And there in the background at Sydenham was my grandfather, Owen Chilton Goodenough Hayter. He must have been in his fifties then. He was a friendly presence, even though I don't remember much about him from that time. I know he was quite at ease in that household, because he was always at ease — a comfortable, low key, confident person, not tall, but compact and attractive, with deep set, bright blue eyes and a lovely smile. I didn't know then how knowledgeable he was — how he would be another person who would answer questions seriously. That would happen much later, though by then I had lost the ability to ask the questions I really wanted answered.

I know I felt close to my Hayter grandparents even at that early age.

It wasn't till later that I got to know them well and to love them even more. By then they had left the Sydenham house. It remains a blurred but happy memory in my mind.

Questions

There were so many things that simply didn't get talked about in those days — or in our family. Religion was one. My mother did teach us the Lord's Prayer, and we sometimes said it before bed, or rather in bed, because we never went through the kneeling ritual. And there was also the "God bless" litany — "God bless Daddy, God bless Mummy" — and so on through grandparents and any one else we might choose. That was all — it was a sporadic system, and it didn't include any instruction on the Bible or Jesus or the Ten Commandments and such. When I discovered about the Crucifixion I was fascinated by it, and wanted to read all about it. I think someone gave us a book of Bible stories, but I know she never read it to us. I had to wait until I could read it myself.

She seemed embarrassed by questions about God or Jesus. Certainly her parents never went to church, though they lived right next to one. We sometimes did go, but only when my father was home. I think he was more of a believer, maybe because he had sometimes faced death. Also, unlike her, he had been to boarding school and had doubtless been exposed to daily chapel and church on Sundays. He sang the hymns lustily, and seemed quite at home in church. I found the service puzzling and mostly incomprehensible. "Why can't I tell him?" I whispered loudly, after one of the vicar's frequent rhetorical questions. "Hush, darling — and do stop grunting!" something I often did when bored. My father called me 'Little Um' because of this habit!

When I asked my mother, during my crucifixion obsession, if the reason she didn't like the Jews was because they killed Jesus, she was too embarrassed to answer. She had, of course, no idea! It was true that there were whole groups of people that in theory she did not like — foreigners, Jews, the wealthy, most officials, Catholics. "Bloody foreigners!" she would mutter, on hearing some rumor about the nefarious doings of some Frenchman or Arab. That was, until maybe she discovered that the nice young man who might be dating her niece was Spanish or Jewish or Hungarian, perhaps even wealthy! or the kind and friendly man was a Catholic. They were then accepted without question or comment — just ordinary people. The Dutch, Africans and Chinese were somehow acceptable anyway, even without being known. It was all inexplicable — obviously the purest form of prejudice, entirely without reason.

Religion, in any case, meant the Church of England — the only kind that implied respectability. It was necessary to conform to some degree, but not to be outwardly holy — nor to discuss such things. None of us were baptized — it was something that was somehow forgotten in our mobile, non church going lives. But that led to an embarrassing situation later on, when we needed baptismal certificates in order to go to our formally Church of England boarding schools. Our mother rounded us up, and took us all to a church where none of us knew the vicar. He tried to test us on our Biblical knowledge, which was minimal, then asked us to sing our favorite hymn. The only one we knew by heart was "Onward Christian Soldiers" which we usually sang rather derisively. But apparently we qualified as C of E members, and he anointed us with the proper words and holy water. So we were quite respectable when we went off to our various schools.

Oddly enough, I eventually liked going to church. It had to be an old and beautiful church, preferably with a good organ and a choir. That was because I'd inherited, or learned from, my parents' love of history and interest in ancient buildings. They had also introduced us to good music, and loved to sing themselves. We had records ranging from Beethoven through Gilbert and Sullivan to Fats Waller. Paul Robeson singing 'Ole Man River' was a part of our lives, and we knew most of the Gilbert and Sullivan songs by heart. That's because we didn't have many records, so we played them over and over. And my mother liked to sing hymns — not the evangelical ones like 'Onward Christian Soldiers', but 'Abide with me' and 'We plough the fields and scatter, The good seed on the land.'

So I was primed to enjoy the lovely medieval churches in the places we lived, with their carved tombs and recumbent statues of knights and ladies, dogs sleeping at their feet. I loved listening to the clear sounds of the choir singing, especially anthems like "Thou Visiteth the Earth", and the thundering organs. The words of the Book of Common Prayer, like "We have erred and strayed like lost sheep" aroused pictures in my mind, and have stayed with me ever since. There was no need to believe anything — one could just enjoy, and remember to get up and down at the right times, and look as if one was praying.

Sunday School, for us, was not an option. That was for 'village children'. Why were village children different? Nobody explained that either. Nobody we knew talked about them, though we saw them every day, tearing round their concrete playgrounds at the village school, and making more noise than we were ever allowed to do. They talked differently from us — dropped their Hs, said "Pardon" instead of "Excuse me", "Me Mum" instead of "My mother". They wore funny caps and big clumsy shoes and socks that were always slipping down to their ankles. They rushed around the streets unguarded, kicking balls, chasing each other, never seeming to go for walks with their mothers. Even though nobody told us not to, we knew we were not meant to talk to these children, and they certainly never talked to us. But we heard them, and wondered.

Other perpetual queries were to do with sex, or even simple questions about our anatomies. My mother had no qualms about nudity. We had baths together until I was about ten, ranged according to age in the bath tub, with me in the privileged position at the back and Richard under the drips. Amazingly, I think this arrangement lasted without much protest until my mother informed me that I was "Too big" to have baths with my brothers — a statement that I took quite literally. Any visiting children were also subjected to scrub downs in the bath tub if we'd all completely covered ourselves with mud — none of them objected and nor did their parents.

So I was quite familiar with the anatomy of male children. In one respect my brothers were different from each other, however. Howard's 'woggle' looked different from Richard's. Of course I wanted to know why — maybe they did too, but I don't remember them asking. It wasn't until I had a baby boy myself that I suddenly realized that Richard had been circumcised! Presumably by the time he was born it had become almost automatic for boy babies to suffer this trauma, but I think it must have demanded quite a bit of pressure for my mother to accede to fashion. She believed in her own judgment when it came to child-care, and would never have chosen to subject her child to pain unless she was persuaded it was absolutely necessary. Of course, she didn't answer my question!

Anything to do with our 'private parts' came too close to the dangerous topic of reproduction, which she was never able to bring herself to describe. I ask "What's this, Mum?" pointing at my genitalia. "Oh, it's just your body, darling," she says vaguely. From then on I avoid the word 'body'. There is obviously something dangerous, even disgusting, about it. The tone of her voice tells me that.

Yet it was only talking about sexual matters that bothered her, not the practice. When I remember her with my father it was obvious she'd enjoyed sex. She breastfed all of us, in front of us and anyone in the family, at a time when most women were giving it up in favor of bottle feeding. She spoke with scorn about this practice. "Bottle fed babies are fat and smelly" she'd say — and in fact, when we looked at them, it was often true. They had huge, shiny, droopy cheeks, and big, fat arms and legs — not nice, compact little bodies and pretty faces like our baby sister Sarah, when she came along. But as with so many things, we didn't know how Sarah came to be until we were much, much older.

Our mother's reluctance to talk was just a minor frustration then, nothing that really affected our enjoyment of life. We had so much else to enjoy. Later it was different.

Brothers and Others

Howard — my closest relative, only sixteen months younger than me — 'Howdie John', then just 'Howdie' — my friend and constant companion, so different from me, but so close — the one I fought with most, but relied on most — the one I treated worst, if only unknowingly — he was one of the several most important people in my life — the only one who called me 'Susie'.

I can tell from the photos my father took that he was a beautiful little boy, flaxen haired and blue eyed, with a lovely smile. Of course I never saw him that way. In fact, until I was about eight I never 'saw' him at all — he was just there, available to do whatever I wanted him to do. Except that sometimes he wouldn't, and that was when our arguments came in. From a very early age I would plan my day. I can still remember some of those plans. I'm lying in bed in the morning, still too sleepy to get up, but thinking of the day ahead. Today, I thought, I'm going to make a basket. Grandpa has pruned the apple trees — there are all those nice whippy sticks to weave it together." And I'd jump out of bed all full of enthusiasm about the day. Like most of my plans, it was abandoned rather fast — my skills didn't match my ambitions. But it shows that I was a bit compulsive about organizing my day, and Howard didn't always want to fit in with that.

I was more independent. Howard was happy watching my mother cooking, or simply being with her. I got bored, wanted to do things myself. I needed adventure, and even if I couldn't manage much of it I found it through reading. Howard, even before he learned to read, loved books with pictures of animals and nature, not so much stories. These interests lasted all his life. He loved animals and was very protective of them. It sometimes seemed as if Howard liked animals more than people — though when Howard loved people he loved them very much. Unlike me, he loved our Masson grandparents more than our

Hayter ones, and I remember that later, when they came to visit us in Devon, he cried when they left.

Perhaps they gave him attention that he lacked at home. Perhaps he never received the sort of attention I had had from my mother when I was very young. I think that's very likely, given her extreme busyness and her attention to housework and to me.

So perhaps it's not surprising that he occasionally flew into great rages at me, hurling himself upon me with his nail bitten hands digging into my cheeks, his favorite means of punishment. I don't remember my mother ever getting involved in these fights, and I don't think I reported them. But I doubtless incited them. They were usually over quickly, without any adult intervention.

Odd things come to mind — Howard loved butter, and would eat chunks of it if he got the chance. And he hated hot milk, which we never had — in fact we drank very little milk. One family always gave us this at teatime, and Howard would refuse it every time, complaining bitterly about it when we left. At home we children drank water most of the time, with the occasional treat like 'Orange Squash' or 'Lemon Barley Water' which were also served to visiting children. We even had hard cider sometimes at our grandparents', which Grandma Masson didn't seem to realize was alcoholic — but I don't think it did any more than make us sleepy!

Another problem for Howard may have been Richard, who seemed to have been born feeling happy, and was everlastingly cheerful, bouncy and daring. They were almost exactly two years apart. Howard tended to worry, about people, about pets, about doing the wrong things, and had moments of melancholy. And I probably didn't help by having more in common with Richard, who liked doing the same things as I did, and would do all I told him to. His cheerfulness also attracted people. Waitresses, bus conductors, chance encounters of all sorts resulted in pats on the head, even kisses, and admiring comments. I think I was a bit jealous of Richard, and I expect Howard was too.

But despite these little tensions we all got on together remarkably well. We had to — we had no easy access to other children. It wasn't the sort of street where you could go out and play games with other kids, and there were high fences between the houses. Howard and I didn't have any friends. We knew several other children, but never saw enough of them to form strong links. I can actually remember some of them. Louise and Duncan, twin flaxen haired children, lived in a big house with an even bigger garden. We loved the garden, with all its space for playing ball and racing each other, but they had a nanny, with the usual restrictions, the grace before tea, the injunctions about getting dirty, the restrictions on swinging too high.

There was a little girl called Caroline, a chemist's daughter. She lived above the shop, and didn't have a garden at all. But she was friendly and liked dressing up, which my brothers didn't — and I even quite enjoyed her birthday parties. But mostly, I was scared of going alone to birthday parties — usually felt out of place and lonely and wanted to go home.

Richard did have a friend when he was very young — a little boy called Robin who was the son of one of my mother's friends. But unless my mother invited children over, or we were invited to another family's home, we didn't see any other children.

There were two exceptions — our cousins Peter and Simon. Peter was a stocky, sturdy little boy, dark haired and serious, with a sweet smile. He had plenty to be serious about. Peter was about seven when his father died. The neighbor's house where they lodged after that was full of cats, and smelt of them. They just had two rooms, and shared bathroom and kitchen with Miss Headley, an eccentric spinster. Auntie Iris had to go to work at a bank, and Peter was sent off to a boarding school. So the boys had a sad childhood. But before Uncle Rob got really ill they often came over to play with us, and sometimes even spent the night. Occasionally I would be asked to stay over in their house, but on the one occasion I tried it I was terrified by the noisy vacuum cleaner, and ended up going home at bedtime.

When they came over to us it was fun, because I actually had someone with interesting ideas for new games. My dolls became perfect patients for Peter, who had developed an interest in medicine since he had begun to suffer asthma attacks during his father's illness. We never went to the doctor, so we had never thought about operations or laxatives or measles. The dolls experienced all of these.

Later, when Peter was at boarding school nearby, his asthma got even worse, and we would sometimes visit him, a sad little boy wheezing in his bed. But my mother could cheer him up — he was a special favorite of hers, and he loved her too. She could always make him laugh.

Simon was a different matter. He was about Howard's age, and apart from once being very helpful in digging a large pit for an underground house I don't remember much about him. This was probably not fair, because I was influenced by my mother, who once said that Simon tormented animals. This little item bore a lot of weight, since we had a cat and a tortoise and were fiercely protective of them. I was suspicious of Simon for a long time.

The death of their father changed these boys' lives in ways that can't all be determined. But when our mother developed cancer we were luckier. The National Health System had been introduced, and all her treatment was covered. Since we were all under 18 this was a blessing for us, and the contrast in experiences influenced my views for ever.

Looking back, I can see it was a big advantage to have plenty of time and freedom to organize at least part of our days. Since we didn't go to school at this point we were pretty unscheduled — and nobody tried to 'entertain' us. We invented our own games, and one thing I don't remember is ever being bored.

Talk of War

A dults always assume children don't listen when they're talking about serious, grown up affairs. But we probably spent more time with our parents, grandparents and other adults than many middle class children like us in the 30s. We didn't have almost separate lives like children with nannies, who often only saw their parents a couple of times a day, and weren't constantly exposed to adults joking, arguing, speaking in hushed voices — which of course aroused our curiosity. My mother often had friends over for tea or coffee, especially when my father was away, as he was for two whole years from 1937 to 1939. They would sit in the 'drawing room' and gossip, but gradually their voices would lower, they would start surreptitiously glancing over their shoulders to see where we were, and the word 'war' would recur. I was usually the one who heard, because I used to draw or read, sitting on the floor behind the sofa.

There was no laughter then — no long stories. The voices were quiet and hesitant — there was fear and uncertainty in them. The words 'air raid shelters', 'gas', 'sirens', 'evacuation' came up, over and over. The last one provoked my mother's indignation. "There's no way they're going to take my children anywhere!"

"But what about bombs, Gene? Would you want them to get bombed?"

"Of course not. But they're better off being with me, even if we do get bombed."

The word 'bomb' aroused more fear in me than any of the others. What was this thing that they were all afraid of? The fear was enough to make me call out from behind the sofa "What are bombs?"

There was nervous laughter. Then one of them said "They blow houses up, dear" I could feel my mother's disapproval of this answer, which was much too close to the truth to please her. She would have

40

preferred a much vaguer description, or none at all. But in fact the answer was rather reassuring. I imagined a house literally blown upwards, and floating calmly back to earth. It didn't sound too bad at all.

A name became familiar — in fact several names. One was Hitler (bad) and another Churchill (good) and one called Ribbentrop, who seemed to be important but not as bad as Hitler. We heard their names on the radio, too, in the six o'clock BBC news that my mother tried to listen to. She listened intently, and didn't want us to interrupt.

Apart from the war talk, our lives continued as usual during this time, but without our father's visits. There was a holiday at the beach on Hayling Island, when it seemed to rain every single day, and at the end, when we were leaving the rented cottage we'd stayed in with Georgie, Richard's chamber pot fell off the top of the taxi and rolled across the road. A better holiday was a year later when our mother took us to Sandown in the Isle of Wight, without Georgie this time, and we stayed in a boarding house in the center of town. There were other children there, but we were sent to bed at our usual early hour, about six thirty, I think, and could hear the other kids playing outside, with the sun still shining in through the thin curtains. Apart from that frustration it was a blissful time. We went to the beach every day — running together across the tide rippled sand and splashing in the small waves, digging holes and building forts, watching a 'Punch and Judy' show, all gathered around a little striped tent with a stage on top, where two horrible puppets battered each other and screamed in a way we could never have done. We went out in a fast motor boat, which leant far too much on its side as it swerved round in circles. And we searched without success for the silver crowns that had been buried in the sand by the town managers.

I even made a friend on the beach, something I had never done before — a little girl who jumped up and down in the waves with me, holding my hand tightly.

Down the street from the boarding house was an ice cream shop where they had green ice cream. I longed to try it, but my mother, always nervous about strange foods, wouldn't buy it for me until the very last day — and then it was a disappointment — tasteless and boring. But it was good to try something new. Going home was sad, and that evening I cried. "What's the matter, darling?" my mother asked.

But I couldn't tell her. It was the first in a series of desolations I felt on leaving places where we'd all been happy, where my mother wasn't busy all the time, when we had fun together. I had never realized before that people could be different in other situations, and that 'away' could sometimes seem better.

Another 'away' — when my mother was not relaxed. It must have been the end of August 1939. We had gone to stay with our Hayter grandparents in Devon, where they'd moved to a small house on a country lane in Budleigh Salterton. Now that all their children had moved away my grandmother had wanted to be near her two sisters, who had moved there when their husbands retired from their jobs in India. Budleigh was full of old India hands, mostly Indian army, with a sprinkling of other professions. It was the first time we'd been to this house. It was smaller than our house, with two little attic bedrooms upstairs, into which we all crammed. And as usual, there were uncles and aunts and cousins, all now staying in hotels or with other relatives in the area.

The aunts and uncles were digging a hole, a big one, in the front lawn. I can see them now, a line of legs and bottoms, all with spades, plunging them furiously into the sticky red Devon clay, hurling it into heaps behind them. Every now and then one of them would draw him/herself upright, pull out a handkerchief and wipe his/her brow. They talked, they laughed, they teased each other — they quoted bits of poetry and occasionally used foreign words I didn't understand. "What are they doing?" I whispered to my grandmother, who was not taking part in this strange activity. She glanced towards my mother, who was just standing there, her lips tight, her eyes not smiling. "It's just a shelter — or — a place where people can go if…" My mother grabbed my hand. "Time for your walk, darling" she said firmly.

I never did get an answer to my question. Our uncles and aunts must have been told not to mention the scary words 'War' or 'Air raid Shelter'. We were to be protected from dangerous knowledge.

I wonder now how many parents refused to talk to their children about the fears that pervaded their own thoughts. Perhaps a lot, because it's a natural impulse to try to protect one's children from fear. It doesn't work. Of course children take in much more than adults ever realize, and hidden dangers often seem worse than those that can be explained. And even if they're pretty bad in reality, it's better to face them together.

But that visit introduced me to the wonders of really living in the country, of walking on beautiful high red cliffs and wading on beaches consisting of wonderful smooth pebbles, — of having the freedom to explore the fields behind our grandparents' house all on our own. The visit came to an end when my mother must have heard that my father would soon be home from China — or perhaps that was just an excuse. I know that was what my grandmother told me as I sat on my bed while she helped me put on my white sandals. Perhaps I was crying. She was trying to explain to me why we had to go.

Reading

On April 9 1939 I became six years old. My father sent me an airmail letter with drawings of me and my birthday cakes through the years, ranging from chubby toddler with fat knees to a fairly normal looking girl standing by an enormous birthday cake. The only present I remember was a large and gaudy brooch, given to me by some not very well known neighbor. I loved it and felt very grown up. I'm sure I had other presents — my mother was good at birthdays. They started on her bed in the morning, surrounded by gifts, including some for the ones whose birthday it wasn't. That was so that nobody felt left out. But the brooch, and what happened next day, are what stuck in my mind.

I never have discovered why I didn't go to school. Six was the usual starting age. Perhaps there was no local school that my parents liked. Maybe it was the approach of the Second World War. Perhaps they decided that a child so shy that she always had to be fetched home early from birthday parties wouldn't survive whole days among scheming little girls.

Whatever the case, the day after my sixth birthday a middle aged lady clad in a rust colored coat and skirt rolled up to our house on an ancient black bicycle, swung one foot over the other to dismount, picked up a pile of books from the bike basket, and strode to our door.

I was waiting for her. I'd met her, at the home of her elderly parents, with whom she lived. Her father was a retired vicar in the Church of England. My mother had taken me there to have tea, and presumably to be inspected as a potential pupil. I was impressed by the delicious cakes and beautiful garden. I must have passed the test, and I must have liked Miss Cuddeford, because there she was, and I was about to have my first lesson.

"What would you like to learn first?" she asked as we settled down at the kitchen table. We were all alone in the house. My mother had taken my two brothers out for a walk as soon as she arrived. It was the first time I had ever been alone with a stranger.

"To read" I answered without hesitation. I had been longing to read, almost desperate to read, already reciting poems my mother read to us, knowing whole stories by heart.

Miss Cuddeford pulled a slim blue book from her pile, and we started. The first words I learned were prepositions — "in, on, up" illustrated by a dog in a kennel, a rooster on a fence, a child climbing some stairs. We went on to simple nouns — animals, clothing, household objects — simple three letter words. With each word Miss Cuddeford sounded out the letters, and I put the sounds together.

By the end of that lesson I could read every word we'd covered, and couldn't wait to go on and learn more. I couldn't recite the alphabet, but I knew some letters, and I knew reading was going to be easy.

In time we went on to Writing, Arithmetic, English, History, Geography, Botany, Sewing, French, Drawing, 'Scripture'. This last was a revelation. With Miss Cudddeford I read Bible stories, from Old and New Testaments. I had never heard about Abraham, or David and Goliath, or wealthy King Solomon. Miss Cuddeford, being the daughter of a clergyman, was a little shocked at my ignorance, particularly since I didn't really know who Jesus was. But I was morbidly fascinated by the story of his death and resurrection, much more so than by the lurid tales in the Old Testament. Death was another thing we never talked about at home.

Miss Cuddeford came four days a week, for two hours a day. In those hours I learnt to sew, and made my mother a needle case, yellow felt with red and blue felt flowers sewn on, leaves and stalks in green embroidery thread. We did exercises together, standing by the table and waving our arms around.

Some days Miss Cuddeford brought in pictures for me to copy. I drew them first in pencil then colored them in watercolor — trees and lakes and castles and mountains. I learned that mixing blue and yellow made green, yellow and red made orange, blue and red resulted in purple. I discovered perspective, using a pencil held at arms length to measure the respective sizes of objects before I drew them.

History was fun — stories about Kings and Queens and famous people, with no attempt to remember dates or actual achievements. It was

King Arthur and the Round Table, King Canute holding back the waves, Henry VIII and his six wives. "A very bad man, dear" Miss Cuddeford said. Of course I learned about the Spanish Armada, and Francis Drake playing bowls on Plymouth Hoe as the Armada approached.

Geography covered Red Indians, and Canadian fur traders, and maps of England and the countries of Europe copied from an atlas. It was deserts and tropical forests and huge oceans so wide it took weeks to cross them. Lots of the countries in the atlas were colored red. "That's because they're part of our Empire, dear," Miss Cuddeford told me.

And everything except the 'art' and the sewing involved reading, even arithmetic. A picture of a table laden with 'tea time' food — sandwiches and scones and cakes and biscuits — might have the question under it "There are twelve biscuits on the blue plate. If John takes two and you take five, how many are left?" When I started to learn about currency, there was a picture of a green grocer's store, with the fruit piled up in front, labeled with the prices. How much for a pound and a half of plums — how much for six apples?.

In summer our lessons were moved to the sitting room, which was cooler than the kitchen. The window looked out on the driveway and the front gate, which opened onto the street. The ice cream man pushed his cart along the sidewalk there, ringing his bell as he passed, and casting his eye towards our window. If the time was right, Miss Cuddeford would wave, he'd come to the window and she'd buy us an ice cream apiece — always vanilla in a waxed paper cup, with a wooden spoon tucked under the lid. The wooden spoon seemed to add to the flavor, and if I ever have one today it still does.

My mother and Auntie Iris called Miss Cuddeford Phyllis. They had known her since they were children. Perhaps they were children together. I didn't think about it — Miss Cuddeford seemed ageless to me, not pretty and young like my mother, or old like my grandmother. I don't remember laughing with her, or misbehaving in any way. She seemed to know everything, and I wanted to learn it. She would correct me gently if I turned a P or an E the wrong way, guiding my hand in my new 'joined up' handwriting. I learned her favorite poems by heart — Yeats' "The Lake Isle of Innisfree" and Sir Henry Newbolt's "The Fighting Temeraire". I can still repeat them today. She was exactly what I needed.

She even took me to church sometimes, to the Children's Service. I discovered that I much preferred the adult version, despite the rhetorical questions. The vicar talked in a special voice to children, as if we were too small to understand anything much. I preferred the organ music and the beautiful, if incomprehensible words of the real service.

I learnt much more than my lessons from Miss Cuddeford. I learnt the word 'selfish', which she applied to me on several very appropriate occasions. It probably applied all the time. Perhaps all children are entirely self centered — I certainly was. It never occurred to me that my adults had feelings much like mine, or even that my brothers did. I certainly knew when they were upset because that could affect the way they treated me, but I didn't feel for them.

It was much easier to feel for people in a book, whose sadness or anger was explicable and described.

When I behaved quite horribly badly after Sarah was born — wouldn't look at her and cried for days — Miss Cuddeford reprimanded me. "You should be happy, Susan," she said severely. "Think how lucky you are to have a darling baby sister. And you must try to help your dear mother!"

But I didn't know how to help, and even now I think Miss Cuddeford's approach to 'selfishness' was wrong. I loved her, though, and I'm eternally grateful for all she taught me — particularly reading. Never again did I have a teacher who measured up to her.

The immediate result of her teaching was that I became enthralled by books. By the end of that year I was reading anything I wanted. I read everything from cereal packages to the newspapers. Since all my relatives gave me books for birthdays and Christmases I was never short of material. And now I was able to read the frightening, mystifying notices that began to appear everywhere — notices that talked about bombs, and gas masks, and air raid shelters. They lurked in the background, something to try to avoid, but which fascinated, and disturbed me.

Books became the counter weight to these worries — I could read them and be away in a different world. I was a bookworm, everyone said, perpetually immersed, at first to my mother's pride, then later to her annoyance. At children's parties I would scan the bookshelves for appealing titles, and settle down in a corner and read — not something that led to social success! I was totally unschooled in little girls' chatter and concerns. But books made parties, which before had terrified me, quite bearable!

The Happy Time

Just before war was declared on September 3 1939 we were all at home when the telephone rang. My mother ran to answer it. And as she spoke I knew that the thing we'd all been looking forward to for ages was happening — my father was home from the China seas! Her face glowed, her voice was full of joy. Right away, a taxi was called, we were bundled into our best clothes, and rushed off to the Portsmouth Town Station.

Across the crowds we spotted him in a telephone kiosk, probably phoning us again. He caught sight of us, spun around, flung the door open and was with us in a flash, his arms wide open to embrace my mother in a long, tight hug. We clung to his legs until he came up for breath and picked us up one by one. He held us close to his slightly bristly, tobacco scented, warm, familiar cheeks, kissed and exclaimed over us — "Little Um!" (his name for me because of my habit of 'umming') — "Howdie John!" ""Roguey Richard!"

I don't remember more — but our family was complete again. We were happy. And exciting things happened. Over the next few months strange boxes were delivered to our house. Some of them were huge, some tiny. They were my father's purchases from China. There was a large green papier mache dragon for Howard. For me and our mother there were papier mache boxes, hers large, big enough to put clothes or blankets in. Mine was much smaller. They were lined with blue cotton fabric, and were perfect for keeping my treasures in — such as my painting equipment and the collection of little blown glass animals that my father had brought me. Both of them were painted all over with scenes from China — beautiful landscapes, ladies in flowing robes with piled up dark hair, houses with curving roofs.

There was another much bigger, heavier delivery, a carved camphor wood chest, which would be filled with all our winter clothes and bedding, so that they smelt deliciously of camphor. And three little tables, carved and polished, that stacked on top of each other in the drawing room from then on. Howard and Richard had model Chinese junks, perfect in every detail, and there were other things we couldn't use but were beautiful and lovely to look at, like a Chinese wedding skirt, blue and pink, pleated all over in tiny, narrow pleats.

My father had a photo of himself dressed up as a Mandarin, seated on a throne — like chair and wearing a drooping moustache. He had loved China, and told us how he used to go out and stay in peasant huts so that he could learn the language.

It was wartime now, but we barely noticed it. My mother put black curtains up over our windows and stuck tape all over the windows, but it didn't scare me because my father was home and everything was going to be all right. There were no air raids — everything seemed normal. And our family was normal again too. It was the so-called 'phony war' — when plenty was happening in Eastern Europe, but not to us. We were fine — we were going on trips with my father — to Eastney Barracks, where he was now stationed, on shopping expeditions to Southsea, on walks in the Downs (which were really 'ups'), to the Lido, where one could rent a boat and go rowing or sail the two model Chinese junks. The junks were not meant to be sailed, which we found out rather soon when they always capsized.

That Christmas was the best one ever. Christmas was always fun, and continued to be, whatever happened, but this one was special. It was the only one where I remember my father being home. As always the house was decorated with holly and home made paper chains. When we woke up in the morning there were heavy lumpy things on the end of our beds, which turned out to be our socks, filled with tiny toys and candy and nuts and oranges, whistles and noise makers. We opened them on our parents' bed, while they drank their early morning cups of tea. When we went downstairs, the Christmas tree, which had miraculously appeared overnight, sparkled with real candles and beautiful spun glass ornaments, and around it were piles of presents.

But we couldn't open them yet. Everything had to proceed according to tradition. After breakfast we had to brush our teeth, and make our beds. We were already dressed in our party clothes. And then the best part came. Our parents must have been feeling celebratory that year. There was a toy ice cream cart for Richard, with toy ice creams inside it. For me there was a perfect 'Bunnykin' tea set — real Doulton china, with tea cups you could really drink from. And for Howard — Howard's was best of all. It was a scooter, a real, solid metal scooter, all ready for the road — and I was madly envious of Howard, for once. But it was too great a day to feel mad long.

Christmas dinner was at noon. We looked forward to it all year. We ate roast chicken with stuffing and roast potatoes and green beans and mince pies and Christmas pudding. You had to be careful with the Christmas pudding, because there were tiny silver threepenny bits baked into it, which might crack your teeth if you were unprepared. Then there were crackers, which you pulled until they split and exploded (I didn't like that part). Inside there were funny paper hats and little toys, mostly whistles or puzzles. Still at the table, we cracked walnuts and hazel nuts and tough, chewy Brazil nuts, ate candied fruit and drank ginger wine. And after all that you could settle down with a book by the fire or play with a new doll or a toy truck or a game. And my father took a photo of us all piled into the old pram we played in, wearing the Chinese skull caps he'd brought home with him. He took it at arm's length with his tiny Zeiss camera, managing to get his own smiling face into it as well. For once there were photographs of us three, though none of my mother. I expect she, as usual, was busy doing something else.

Even after all that there was something more. In the evening, after tea and heavy Christmas fruit cake, there were the Christmas tree candles to light again, and we opened the tiny wrapped gifts hung all over it.

Sometimes at other children's Christmas parties there would be a fairy doll — perhaps really an angel — on top of the tree, and I always hoped against hope that I would be given that doll. Of course I never was — it was just a decoration. Our tree didn't have a fairy doll, or even a Santa Claus, and there was nothing religious about the celebration. But sometimes, after dark had fallen, there would be a knock on the front door, sometimes bold, sometimes hesitant, and a young boy's voice would ask " Carol singers?".

Of course my mother said yes, even though she knew there would be a donation requested at the end. We all piled out into the front garden, and the clear, bright voices of the village kids gathered in the light from the open door would rise on the frosty air in "Hark the Herald Angels Sing " or "Good King Wenceslaus". Of course we joined in — we knew all the carols by heart, because our mother sang them.

Sometimes there were several groups, and after that we were sent off to bed, sleepy and satisfied and loved. Of that we had no doubt, with or without Christmas.

Rochester, and the Best Three Months

I wonder how many children develop the love of places that we three, and later our little sister Sarah did, and I wonder why we did. Why was it that all of us went back and back to the places we loved as children? Sarah, terminally ill in Denmark at the age of 44, too ill to travel, would attempt to run away to England, needing particularly our favorite place on Dartmoor. I suspect I will feel the same. We all, I expect, had later favorite places, but the earlier ones were never forgotten, and retained their magic. For me, Budleigh Salterton, where our Hayter grandparents lived, had begun to assert that pull on me by the winter of 1940, but another place, only known for three short months, remains a blissful memory for all three of us older ones.

Most of our earliest memories were connected to the house we lived in near Portsmouth, on the main road to London in a village called Purbrook. It was still a real village, with a fine church, at least one pub., several shops, and a variety of old houses. But suburbia was already encroaching. It had already swamped Widley, where our grandparents lived, a little closer to Portsmouth. On our side of the busy London Road acres of new housing spread out. Opposite the house, though, were fields and woods, farms and ponds. So we could just cross the road and we were in the country. But we were not allowed to go out the front gate, near the heavy traffic — we could not explore.

Our house, like all the houses my mother chose, was bright and sunny — a cheerful place to be in. Behind it was a wild garden, with a small orchard of apple trees, and just behind the house a large wooden shed, high enough to contain our second swing, very useful on rainy days, and a great place to put on plays, or just to sit and read undisturbed.

We were free to do what we wanted in that garden — dig holes for underground forts, see who could swing the highest, stain our skins with the outer shells of the walnuts that fell from the big tree holding

53

our other swing, climb the apple trees, pick the apples — but none of this led to nostalgic feelings like those we had for "The Old Priory".

It started when our parents, amazingly, actually left us for a few days. This had never happened before, but it can't have been very traumatic, because I can't even remember who looked after us! I do remember them coming back, all excited, talking about the wonderful house they had rented for us in Rochester. Our father had been posted to Chatham, another major Marine base in the neighboring town. This must have been just after our special Christmas, or just before.

They talked about the castle right next to the house, the old Thames barges with red sails on the river below it, the stories that said Anne of Cleves, Henry VIII's fourth wife, had once stayed there. They told me I would really like it, since I loved history so much. They didn't tell us that it still had gas lighting, that the only heating apart from fires was from free standing kerosene stoves scattered dangerously around the house, or that rats scampered through the attic at night, frequently coming down to demolish anything edible. They knew that wouldn't interest us — and I think it didn't interest them too much either. It was a most unsuitable house for three children aged six and a half, five and three, but they had chosen correctly. We loved it from the start, all of us.

As it happens, the winter of 1940 was one of the coldest on record, and it even snowed! The cars driving up the London Road had chains on — you could hear the strange grinding sound as they slowly traveled by. It was our first snow, but we couldn't enjoy it, because we all had a stomach bug on the day we were meant to leave for Rochester, and sat around the drawing room clutching bowls and feeling miserable.

The next day we set off early. Our father, who was already in Chatham, was meeting us in London where we changed trains. A real train journey was also an excitement — especially breakfast in the dining car, with linen table cloths, heavy white china, beautiful brown boiled eggs, and tiny jars of marmalade, one for each of us. There was another reunion under the big clock at Waterloo Station (it's still there) and then off on the short ride to Rochester.

It was nearly dark when we arrived in Rochester — sunset comes early in an English January. From the taxi I could see, lit up in the dim headlights, the gray, forbidding walls of the ancient castle on our right. We stopped on the left side of the road, and walked straight into enchantment.

The hall was dark. My father struck a match and lit the mantle of the gas lamp on the wall ahead of us. Carved oak paneling appeared, dark and shiny, reflecting the flame. We moved onwards, my father lighting the way as we went, to a large dining/sitting room with an enormous fireplace. "Come on, chicks" said my father, "Let's look up the chimney!" So we stood in the fireplace and looked up, and there was the moon above us. It was lucky it wasn't raining!

In our parents' bedroom was a huge four poster bed with blue velvet curtains. Ours seemed quite ordinary until the morning, when we discovered it looked straight out on the castle Keep, built in the 1100s by William Rufus, son of William the Conqueror. The pigeons that lived in its walls woke us each day with their cooing.

But the room that fascinated me and aroused my longing was as close to a fairy tale dwelling as anything could be. 'The Old Priory' was three stories high. Half way up the stairs was a landing, and off the landing a short step ladder led to a little square room built over the stairwell. There was a door, and a window to the left of it. Outside it was whitewashed, in contrast to the dark Tudor paneling that covered all the rest of the house. Inside the room was white also. There were rosebud patterned curtains at the window which looked across the stairwell, then through a big window to the castle. There was just room for a bed and a chair inside.

I wanted nothing more than to have this room for my bedroom, and nagged my parents for weeks until they let me do it. Since I was a child who often got up in the night and looked for them, and since to get to them I had to go down the step ladder in the dark, it was amazing that they eventually gave in — but apparently my joy prevented any night terrors! I don't remember ever climbing down that ladder in the night.

I've discovered that this little room was probably an 18th century 'Powdering Room' — built to fit into the only space available in the ancient house. Here gentlemen — and sometimes ladies — would sit while their wigs were powdered to remove the grease and dirt that would clog them. They had to be wearing the wigs, because otherwise the powder would float off in the struggle to put them on. And it was a messy business — hence the special room.

Anyway, I hope that when the fashion changed and wigs were no longer worn some little Victorian girl enjoyed it as much as I did. Perhaps she was like me, someone who sometimes liked to be alone with her thoughts, her dolls and her books.

"The Old Priory" was, in fact, just part of a very big house, owned by our landlady, Miss Shinkwin. One end of it was called Satis House, the name of Miss Havisham's house in "Great Expectations", and since Dickens lived in Rochester for a while and wrote "Pickwick Papers" there it probably really was the house that had inspired him. But its name was due to a visit by Queen Elizabeth herself in 1573 to the then owner, Richard Watts. In thanking him for his services she used the Latin word 'Satis' to express her satisfaction, and that became its name from then on.

So there was Satis House at one end, heavily restored and rebuilt in sections, and there were two other dwellings, both dating from the early 1500s, one of which was ours for those three months. They had been virtually untouched, except that their interior walls, covered in Tudor paneling, had been covered with plaster at some time in the past. Miss Shinkwin told us she had stripped it off all our walls, and was in the process of doing the same with her own house. Some of hers were painted and apparently almost unique. I was surprised when she said that the paneling was rare and valuable, because it seemed dark and ugly to me, and was the only thing I didn't like about the house.

This was where we were going to live. And there was more to come. A person came with the house, a very small person called Maudie. She was what was called then 'a maid of all work' — but what she really loved to do was bake cakes. I have never, ever smelt anything so tempting as Maudie's cakes, or eaten anything more delicious. They were warm and perfectly flavored, tasting of butter and eggs and good ingredients not masked by too much vanilla or spices, and she iced them and decorated them, something my mother never did.

My mother was a good cook, but didn't like it — it's pretty boring to cook for small children most of the time. So Maudie became more of a cook than a maid, which suited my mother fine. We had never had anyone like Maudie before.

We loved her, and she loved us, especially Richard, who was a charming, cheerful little boy, always bouncing off things and scraping knees and elbows, which Maudie cleaned up for him, clucking sympathetically and kissing the top of his head.

There was another person who became part of our lives at that time. This was a man called Turner — or that was what we called him, because he was my father's 'batman' and that was how officers' servants were addressed. In those days every officer had a servant, chosen from among his men. They looked after their officer's uniforms, polished his shoes, whitened the belt of his dress 'blues'.

This was considered to be a rather privileged position, and certainly Turner behaved as if he thought so. Turner was probably about the same age as my father, and had children of his own, somewhere in England. Batmen were also allowed to help in their officer's homes, and that's how we met him.

He would come over with my father and help with the heavy housework, but he was never too busy to talk to us. He liked to hear about our invented games — the battles we were having with our imaginary enemies, the Bolsters — our explorations of the terraced gardens below our own that led all the way down to the river and were accessed by scary step ladders, and the snow man we built (with his help) when it snowed really hard. He was another adult we loved.

My mother and Miss Shinkwin liked to chat. I can't imagine they had much in common, but my mother could talk with anyone. They probably weren't far apart in age, though Miss Shinkwin seemed ancient to us. She had a trio of Pekineses, noisy little animals who swarmed over the low bank between our gardens and played ball with us. Howard loved them. He had a passion for animals, which lasted all his life.

During this time my father was home a lot, though not all the time. When he was there we would all go over to the castle. In the courtyard there were flocks of pigeons. You could buy a bag of corn, and if you put some on your head a pigeon would perch there and eat it. Howard would let them do this. My parents encouraged us to do daring things — especially my father — and they didn't watch us every minute. We'd climb all over the old World War I tank that was stationed on the edge of the fortifications, and pretend to be taking it into battle. And we'd ride Howard's scooter round the path that ran around the Keep. It was up and down, and once Richard tried the scooter, and it ran away with him going downhill, leading to a fall and more scraped knees.

Sometimes we'd go to the top of the Keep. This meant climbing a scary spiral staircase, its stone steps all worn and slippery, with views down into the dungeon, where, my father would tell us, the prisoners had been kept and subjected to terrible tortures. I didn't like looking down there, and certainly never wanted to take those steps. But at the top, under the open sky, it was glorious. You could look right down on our house, see the river winding around the town, see the cathedral and the green countryside beyond all the houses. We would sit on the low walls between us and open space, and look straight down to the grassy banks surrounding the castle.

My father had a birthday soon after we arrived. My mother took us all to the other side of the river, to an adjoining town called Strood. We walked down the castle hill, and across the bridge, to a little shop that sold pipes. My father loved smoking a pipe — never cigarettes. The shop had ordinary pipes, but also white clay pipes, and that's what my father wanted. We bought two long stemmed pipes, then we children chose another one especially from us. It had a large bowl painted with brightly colored flowers. We never saw him smoking it — he said it was too pretty. But in Rochester he smoked the others, sitting in the elegant upstairs drawing room with tapestry covered chairs that we didn't use very often.

We also went shopping with my father, always to buy presents for my mother, even though it wasn't her birthday. One day it we were looking for slippers. He always let us help him choose, and this time we all chose some high heeled satin-y slippers, a pretty gold color. We watched anxiously as she unwrapped them. She told us she loved them, and kissed us all, especially my father, but I wasn't quite sure she was telling the truth. And another time we went shopping for a hat. I don't know why — perhaps it was intended for the trip they did later. We chose a tiny pill box hat covered with artificial flowers. She was very polite about it, but once again I was doubtful. It was true that I'd never seen her in a hat like that! However, she did wear it when they went off and left us with Maudie, for two nights in London.

They came back laughing and full of stories. They'd gone to a show each night, and brought us two records of the songs they'd heard. The first night they'd stayed at the Mayfair, a very luxurious hotel. I expect they danced — they loved dancing, and sometimes they'd teach Howard and me some steps as we all danced in the living room. But that hotel was too expensive, so the next night they moved to a cheaper place. It sounded as if they hadn't cared — they had fun, and we loved to hear all about it. We played the records for years, both from musicals playing in London at the time. One was the song "My Heart belongs to Daddy" by Cole Porter — which I always thought referred to us. The other was "Run, Rabbit, Run" by Noel Gay., a big hit later on in the war years.

We went to a zoo for the first time, and met an elephant called Lizzie, who shared her stall with a Shetland pony. The attendant told us that elephants need companionship, and the pony was Lizzie's friend. I drew a picture of Lizzie when we got home, in a little notebook with pink covers that I still have. And my father took Howard and me to see our first megalithic monument, two large rocks supporting another one between them. It was called Kit's Coty House. We stood there on that chilly February afternoon, while my father told us about the ancient people who had built it so long ago.

Occasionally we'd go to have tea with our father, brought to us by Turner in heavy white china cups. My father had a room in the high ceilinged old Georgian Barracks at Chatham, and once we even saw the King there. From a window high above the Parade ground we looked down on the massed columns of sailors and marines, all in their dress uniforms, as George VI inspected his troops. It was pouring with rain, and the King was mostly hidden by a large umbrella. I was disappointed that he wore no crown — in fact he was not nearly as handsome as our father.

Sometime before the end of our stay in Rochester my mother started to feel sick each day. She even spent a lot of time in bed. We didn't mind this much, which was different from other times, when Howard and I became sad and worried on the rare occasions when she was ill. Perhaps this was because my father was there most nights, and Maudie was so kind and reassuring.

One evening my mother said she would love some champagne. My father immediately went out to buy some, and we gathered by the blazing fire in the dining room. We children had our first taste, the bubbles

59

tickling our throats. We didn't know that perhaps this was to celebrate my mother's pregnancy with our little sister Sarah, doubtless conceived in the four poster bed with the blue velvet curtains — or perhaps on their romantic trip to London.

I doubt if my mother was really overjoyed at her condition. How could she be, with three small children already, a war going on, and a husband who was always getting shipped off overseas? We had never had a time like this, with my father close by, and a lovely person like Maud to make my mother's life easier. But we were all together, and happy, that night.

Soon afterwards there came a day when my mother looked as if she had been crying. Her eyes were all swollen and red, and she and my father spent a lot of time in their bedroom. As usual, nobody told us what was going on, but I found a torn piece of green wrapping paper, and on it wrote, in my newly learned 'joined up' writing, "I know why you are red. Daddy has got another ship". And I was right.

I have no memory of our departure from the Old Priory — no glimpses of farewells to Maudie or Turner or Miss Shinkwin — nothing about our trip home on the train. Except it didn't feel like home — Rochester had taken its place. And I have only the vaguest recollection of the next several months, even though these contained my seventh birthday.

The memories of that winter in Rochester have remained, clear and remarkably the same for Howard, Richard and me.

Perhaps this shows how much one really does suppress disturbing memories. I don't remember one sad time during our stay in Rochester. There must have been some. I must have been dimly aware of my parents' worries — must have heard words or seen glances that alerted me. Otherwise how could I have known to write that note? But they wanted us to be happy, on what might be our last time together. And we were.

Years and years after the war, almost exactly 30 years since we'd lived in Rochester, I met Turner again. Howard had tracked him down — he was living in a London County Council retirement home on the edge of London. It happened that we were back from America, in London for a meeting. I got on the train one day, and went down to see him.

I picked up some chocolates in a corner shop, and walked through the tidy suburb. The Home was attached to a Primary School — children played in the yard outside. Inside, the place sparkled. There were fresh flowers on every surface. A friendly attendant brought Turner to me — a stocky, weather beaten man with a huge smile on his face. He crushed me to his warm brown woolen sweater. Tears came to my eyes — perhaps to his also.

In his little room we talked about my father, about his love of boxing, his letter writing, his knitting (he knit little vests for Sarah while on the Bonaventure). Turner (Bill, as I now called him) remembered our snowman, and the fun we had together. Most of all, he remembered my mother with obvious respect and affection. He told me how worried he had been about her during and after the war, how he had lost touch with us when we moved to Devon, as we had lost touch with him.

He died two months after I met him. His son said our meeting had meant a lot to him. It did for me too. And for me it confirmed my memories.

When the War Really Came to Us

The boys and I were playing on the front lawn one day that summer. It was a clear, sunny day — no clouds in the sky. All of a sudden there were two planes above us, swooping and climbing, seeming to chase one another. They were tiny, far up, glinting as the sun caught their wings. They left white tracks behind them, a pattern of swirls in the blue. There wasn't much sound — they were too far up.

In one instant they were playfully painting their tracks, in the next one of them was diving, rotating, towards the woods below, a cloud of black smoke following him. There was a distant boom as he disappeared into the trees. More smoke rose. My mother ran out of the house and pulled us back inside. "It's all right, chicks!" she said. " That was a German plane — good thing they got him!"

But how did she know? We could hardly see those planes — they were much too far away. And of course we weren't alarmed at all — it was really exciting. Once more she wanted to make sure that we weren't upset. But that was our first direct experience of war.

I vaguely remember being fitted with gas masks and finding them uncomfortable, smelly and scary. The idea of actually having to wear one was terrifying. We did, very soon, discover that one could make realistic farting noises from inside a mask, so that was one consolation! They came in brown cardboard boxes with straps so you could carry them, which we were meant to do at all times — but I don't think we did. If we'd gone to school at this time we would have had to take part in air raid drills, which might have either amused me or terrified me, given my ability to imagine the worst situations. But we were safely at home with our mother and Miss Cuddeford, so weren't subjected to such possible traumas. My mother, who mistrusted government and officialdom in any form, tended to laugh at such precautions. She did stick tape back and forth across all our windows, and had our tiny cellar reinforced with strong wooden beams. And she was careful to draw the heavy 'black out curtains' tightly every evening.

That summer was not like the one before — no holiday at the beach, no visit to our grandparents in Devon, no haymaking picnics out at Mr. Plair's farm. Instead my mother was sick a lot. A lady called Florence came over and took us for our afternoon walks. Walks with Florence were boring. She preferred to walk along the streets. There were no visits to the cow shed, no dam building in the stream, no tree climbing in the woods. Miss Cuddeford was a consolation, though she had no sympathy for my dislike of Florence, or for my impatience with my mother's afternoons in bed. None of us, of course, had any idea why she was sick.

But now that I could read everything I buried myself in books, almost imbibing the childrens' magazine called Sunny Stories put out by author Enid Blyton, or her exciting stories about treasure hunting and boarding school life. I avoided my mother's old books, which seemed mostly to be about sad little orphans with dying brothers or sisters. Eventually, of course, the orphans were rescued by some wealthy relative who appeared out of the blue, and lived happily ever after, but I couldn't stand the preceding gloom. There was enough gloom in our house, and in any case I had always hated sad books.

But luckily there were other books at hand, and I read them all.

Once, at least, that summer my father came home. I can remember his arrival so distinctly that I think it can only have happened once. I'm having my lessons with Miss Cuddeford. Someone comes in the front door — I can't see, because it's summer and we're in the drawing room. The front door opens into the dining room to one side of us. Then someone runs up the stairs, and I hear his voice. I shoot out of my chair, ready to dash upstairs after him, but Miss Cuddeford slows me down. "No, dear" she says. "Just let your parents have a little time together" and I wait, unwillingly, a very few minutes, until she lets me go. And I rush upstairs, and into their room, and there he is, in his uniform, and I hurl myself on him and hug him tight. My arms just reach his polished brown leather belt.

I can still see that belt, but after that my memory fades. I imagine Miss Cuddeford came up to get me — she had a better understanding than I did of my parents' needs. But the joy stays with me.

Perhaps it was on that visit that he took me to see the ancient castle at Porchester. It dates from Roman times, but had been added to and adapted over the centuries. I was disappointed in it. There was no tall Keep as Rochester had — no gloomy dungeon. Even being with my father couldn't compensate for its inferiority in my eyes.

He was stationed at Gourock, in Scotland, while the Bonaventure was being built, fitted out, and the crew assembled. She was launched in April 1939, commissioned in May 1940 and escorting liners to Canada by July. In August she was mostly in Scotland being prepared for Atlantic convoy service. So this visit must have been in August, on some brief leave. There's a photo of us up on the Downs at Goodwood, my mother obviously pregnant, so I think this must have been at that time.

Another photo shows us that summer. We children were clustered around her, myself almost twined around her, clinging to her hand. We appear happy — we're smiling and cheerful, looking into the camera. My mother is grim faced, rigid. Who took that photo, I wonder? Was it my father? And perhaps she was angry with him. I have always thought that she wanted him to protest to the Admiralty about the fact that he'd been sent to sea so soon after his two years away. Maybe he did — maybe he was turned down. It was, after all, the beginning of the war. But I suspect that he didn't. While something of a maverick, he was also intensely loyal and patriotic. And he loved adventure.

But perhaps I'm completely wrong, and she was just miserable, lonely, sick and probably frightened, with us three to worry about and another baby on the way.

And the war was warming up fast. Her beloved Holland had been invaded. Denmark and Norway were invaded on my seventh birthday. And those planes circling the sky on that sunny August day were the first signs we had of the Battle of Britain, when Hitler's Luftwaffe attacked the airfields of Britain, and then the coastal cities.

To the immediate east of us were many airfields, mostly Royal Air Force fighter bases where aircraft could be close to the English Channel and be ready to attack any German raiders. As long as it was only airfields that were being attacked we didn't really notice anything much. They weren't far away from us — probably the closest was about fifteen miles away — but although we may have heard distant explosions I don't think we were scared.

We were in bed one night when the sirens sounded. We'd got used to that melancholy wailing sound, warning of a possible raid. So far nothing had happened, and an hour or so had always ended with the reassuring single long drawn out note, sinking to a whisper at its end. This night, though, there were soon thuds in the distance, and the windows rattled. My mother came and pulled us out of our warm beds. This must have been before the cellar was finished, because we all went and sat on the stairs, which were protected from flying glass by a door at the bottom.

The explosions came closer and closer. We could feel them. The house shook, and the windows rattled so much I thought they would break. There were planes overhead, the sound of their engines advancing and retreating, whining and roaring. My mother got up suddenly and rushed to the bathroom, leaving us alone for a moment on the stairs, lit only by a flashlight. She came back white faced and wiping her mouth with a sheet of toilet paper. "It's only our guns firing, chicks," she said — but I knew better.

In a little while the awful sounds faded and disappeared, the wonderful 'All clear' sounded, and we went back to bed. During the day, and every day, our routines continued as usual. The cellar was finished, and we descended there almost every night that late summer and autumn.

In a month or so, Hitler had discovered that his air force was no match for the young British airmen and their motley collection of ancient and recently built aircraft. Britain had been saved from invasion, though that wasn't fully realized yet, and the church bells that were meant to be rung only in the case of invasion were silenced until the end of the war. What had been a lovely, joyful sound was now something to be dreaded. But what happened immediately after the mostly accidental bombing that civilians had experienced during the Battle of Britain changed into the purposeful destruction of cities. This evolved into pretty much random attacks on any village, any farmhouse or railway bridge, that the German pilots noticed. And bomb aiming was certainly not accurate, so that far more than the major targets were hit, and nowhere was really safe.

Portsmouth was actually the first British city to be bombed, largely because of its Naval Dockyard and other military establishments. The first raid was on July 17 1940, when a small group of German bombers swooped down one day and dropped bombs across a wide swathe of the city. I have no idea if this was the day I remember — probably not, because night raids didn't start until later. Britain's sea ports became Hitler's main target once the attacks on airfields had failed to destroy the Royal Air Force. Nearly 1000 people were killed in Portsmouth, and a tenth of its housing was destroyed. All of these ports were heavily bombed, mainly in the early period from 1940 through 1941, but intermittently all through the war.

We were some way out of Portsmouth — at least five miles. But the bombers often dropped their loads miles off target, or if they were being pursued and wanted to get rid of them. So our little village and all the surrounding villages and farmland were subject to sudden attacks, and in any case lived through nights and days of constant air raid warnings and 'all clears'.

I was only seven. I probably remember that autumn as being even worse than it was. I know that it can't have been as bad as it was for people living in Portsmouth itself or London and the other cities. But for a child who had been afraid of fireworks because of their loud noises, and would even run terrified from a train track when a train went thundering by, it was a horrifying experience.

My mother was terrified too. She never outwardly showed it, but I must have felt it. And long afterwards her sister Iris told me how frightened my mother had been, and how sometimes my brave but difficult grandmother had walked all the way in the night to be with her — something I don't remember at all.

What I remember is the house shaking and groaning around us, the dust dropping down from our cellar ceiling, the awful roar of the planes overhead and the whistle of falling bombs. It was easy to distinguish the German bombers — their unsynchronized engines went 'Thump, thump, thump' in a sinister rhythm. I needed to listen all the time — I couldn't talk in case something happened that I needed to hear. And meanwhile my mother made shadow animals on the wall with her flashlight, tried to get us to sing, told us funny stories. Somehow her bravery never transmitted itself to me — I was stuck in a huddle, shivering, barely breathing. But I knew I couldn't cry or express my fear. We were meant to be brave. I waited desperately for the 'All Clear', when we trooped off to bed again.

That autumn there were so many night raids that we all became sleep deprived. It got so bad that my mother decided sleep was more important than a rather doubtful safety, and for a while we slept on mattresses in the drawing room, behind the sofas to protect us from flying glass. I became superstitious, feeling that if I slept in a certain position every night the bombers wouldn't come. But of course they did.

My mother became irritable, quick to anger. Once a neighbor who had become an Air Raid Warden arrived on our doorstep to tell her that a crack of light was showing at one of our windows. He ended by asking sanctimoniously "Don't you know there's a war on?" A fatal mistake! She knew only too well. And not only that, the warden was an apparently able bodied male, about the same age as my father, and he was not off fighting the Germans! She never spoke to him again. Unfortunately, I had just made friends with his daughter, who lived a few houses away, and I never saw her again either.

One day I was reading peacefully downstairs in the drawing room. This was unusual — we almost always stayed upstairs in our nursery. Howard and Richard were playing. Richard got bored with their game, and started jumping around the room on the furniture. Suddenly there was a crash — he had jumped too far, and landed against the window. My mother rushed in from the kitchen, and snatched him up from the floor. I don't think he was even crying — he seldom did — but my mother was red with fury, not so much with Richard, who appeared to be uninjured, but because of the broken window, and my lack of attention to his activities. She marched over to me, slapped me hard across my bare legs, and told me it was all my fault.

Perhaps I wouldn't have remembered this particular incident if I'd ever been asked to look after Richard, but I never had. My mother never, at any time, asked us to take care of our younger siblings. And she had never slapped us.

Now I can understand her reactions perfectly well. They were a direct result of the tensions of war and pregnancy, of being alone and being afraid, of being overworked and busy. But there was nobody to explain this to us, not even our grandparents, who were a real haven at this time. We would go over there one afternoon a week, go for a walk with Grandpa and Whiskey, then listen to the BBC's 'Childrens' Hour', through which I discovered most of my favorite books. It was familiar and comforting over there, in their little house with the fire blazing and Grandma's cakes for tea, and Grandpa telling his own stories. But they were careful to follow my mother's rules for us — or else, perhaps, they had been their own rules too.

I think they loved us more than any of their other grandchildren, perhaps because our mother had been their favorite. They were always pleased to see us, always happy to spend time with us.

Grandpa let us play in the old touring car he had in the garage. I can feel us all, on the smooth, soft, sweet smelling leather seats, driving off for fantastic pretend expeditions to far off places. The rain would often be pouring down outside, for these expeditions were a substitute for our walks, and instead of rolling hills or green forests we were surrounded by Grandpa's carpentry projects. The garage was also his workshop, where once he made a cradle for my dolls and a beautiful dresser with cupboards and cup hooks for my tea set.

I don't think he had ever driven the car himself. He'd bought it, so I was told, for our Uncle Fred, the oldest son, before Fred had gone off to work in Shanghai. Now Fred was interned by the Japanese — not that we knew that. I wonder how much my grandparents knew about where he was. They too must have lived in worry, and not just about Fred. They loved my father too.

And they were also in danger. They were even closer to Portsmouth than we were — very close to the old forts on the top of Portsdown Hill. They had been built to protect against Napoleon's armies. Now they had been taken over by our army. Howard was once out for a walk with my grandfather near a fort when a German plane zoomed over, firing its cannons. They had to dive into a ditch with Scottie dog Whiskey, the one we'd owned as a puppy. And we were walking with Grandpa across the fields opposite Rosyth one day when the siren sounded — Grandpa said nothing, but hastened his stride, and kept glancing fearfully upwards. Luckily we reached a shelter before the distant sounds of explosions echoed across the countryside.

My mother distrusted public shelters, perhaps justifiably. We were all meant to use them when the sirens went off while we were out, but she'd seen them being built, and knew how shoddy their construction often was. And she had no faith in official pronouncements. The shelters were also cold, damp and smelly. So when my father came home on one of his flying visits and we were all out walking when the sirens sounded she immediately made for home. "Shouldn't we go to a shelter?" he asked, sounding a little nervous. I was surprised — I thought he was always brave. "Better off at home!" my mother said cheerily. My father was used to being able to fight back, and told my mother he found it much more alarming to be under attack and not able to retaliate, as he could in sea battles.

The war became evident in the area around us. The old 'Leopard Inn' down the road was bombed and burnt to a shell. A landmine, dropped by parachute, left an enormous crater right next to the home of one of our mother's friends. Several houses were left with a wall missing, so that you could see the rooms inside. Sometimes they looked almost untouched, with clothes still hanging in a wardrobe, or a table with tablecloth, perched on the edge of a floor that disappeared just beyond it. The fields opposite were pitted with craters, which rapidly filled with murky water in the rainy English autumn. And boys went round collecting shrapnel from the anti aircraft shells fired by our guns.

My brothers found some too — twisted, jagged pieces of metal that could tear you apart if they hit you. There wasn't anything my mother could do to prevent us seeing evidence of what war could do. As usual, she didn't explain anything. But she must have told our father of my fear, because he wrote me a letter telling me how brave our airmen were, and how they were up there protecting us from 'the nasty old Germans'. It didn't make much difference — I didn't really connect the noises with people, of either side. And the brave airmen didn't seem to be helping too much.

Of course, none of this compared with the terrible things that were happening to people in occupied Europe, or even with the inhabitants of central cities in Britain. I never saw a dead body, or even knew anyone who was killed in a raid. Mine was the problem of a child with too vivid an imagination. It was too easy to wonder what happened if one of those sharp, twisted pieces of metal hit you, or to think of being buried in the ruined houses we saw, or burnt up in a place like the Leopard. I could not shake these thoughts from my mind, not even when reading, or swinging in the garden on a normal, peaceful day. There was too much to remind me. And I couldn't talk about it either. I tried not to look at photos in the newspaper, or listen to the BBC six o'clock news when my mother had it on. But it was hard not to hear things that scared me. And privately I started to pray every night that the war would end soon.

I wish I knew if my brothers were as scared as I was. I never asked them, never thought about them. But Howard tells me now he was not afraid, but rather excited. I'm not sure if I believe him.

We played together every day as we always had, outside in the mornings, a walk in the afternoon. Our games became warlike — we invented enemies, and stalked them through the orchard. We dropped bombs from the branches of the apple trees, and built our own air raid shelter out of abandoned bricks and wood left over from the cellar roof. We sang songs to the tunes of hymns or popular songs — I remember "We're going to fight the Da, we're going to fight the Da —" to the tune of the Royal Marine song "A Life on the Ocean Wave, a life on the Rolling Deep", sung, as the Marines did, while marching bravely along. And I remember a rhyme about the only two Germans whose names we actually knew, beginning "Hitler and Ribbentrop agreed to fight a war —" which of course was the only thing we knew about them. We knew nothing about the causes of the war, nothing about Nazism or fascism — we just knew that Germans were bad, and that we had to beat them.

A Baby Sister

Our sister Sarah was born on November 10 1940, on one of the few nights that autumn when there wasn't an air raid. The doctor suggested she should be called 'Sirena Bombastina' in memory of the sounds that accompanied her time in the womb. A few days earlier a strange lady, called Mrs. Beets, had inexplicably come to live in our attic bedroom. I didn't like her — I didn't like anyone who seemed to be trying to replace our mother. I don't think my mother liked her much either. She never liked being told what to do, and Mrs. Beets was always telling her to go and lie down or put up her feet or stop dusting the furniture. My mother just went on doing whatever she was doing, and took no notice. So we probably copied our mother, and I don't suppose Mrs. Beets liked us either.

That night the boys and I were sound asleep in the bedroom we shared. I was wakened suddenly by a strange male voice upstairs. There was light coming through the crack under the door, and people were moving around. What was happening? Had burglars got into our house? I got up to see what was going on, trying not to wake the boys, and cautiously, quietly opened the door. All the lights were on. There was a smell of Dettol, the disinfectant that my mother used in the bathrooms, and the murmur of voices downstairs. My mother's door was open. I tiptoed across the landing, so that the burglars wouldn't hear, and into her room. And the first thing I saw was a baby's cradle, a wicker basket with a white, frilly lining, and suddenly I knew what was happening. "You're going to have a horrible baby!" I shouted.

I hardly had time to get to my mother before Mrs. Beets came pounding up the stairs, grabbed me, pushed me back into our room, and locked the door. I was stuck in the dark, more frightened than I had ever been.

I stood there by the door for what seemed like hours. Perhaps it was because I was crying that I didn't hear much of what was going on. But my mother must have tried to labor quietly, knowing we were all next door, and I never heard any moans or cries.

After a long time I heard the doctor going downstairs. Mrs. Beets came and opened the door and took me in to my mother. I ran straight to her, not even looking into the cradle. She held out her arms and I went into them. And I stayed there the rest of the night. I remember the strange, unfamiliar smells, of the rubber undersheet and the disinfectant and maybe blood, but I don't remember anything my mother might have said to me, and I never asked about the baby. It was enough to be with my mother.

She was brave and gallant and kind, but why had she never told us, even in an indirect way, that we were going to have a baby sister or brother? None of us remember being prepared in any way. Howard and Richard were happy and fascinated by the baby. I was already feeling abandoned by my mother's apparent illness and partial absence from our normal lives, plus the terror I felt each night and wasn't able to share. I deeply resented Sarah, and would have nothing to do with her. It seemed to me that she had stolen my mother. The time after her birth was probably the unhappiest in my childhood, even worse than what came later. I cried a lot, and tried to please my mother in new ways. I embroidered a handkerchief for her in the stitches I'd just learnt from Miss Cuddeford, hoping that this might bring her back to the person she had been.

One night she was bathing Sarah in her portable bathtub by the fire. I was crying quietly. My mother looked up. "What's the matter, darling?" she said.

"It's just my eyes watering." I answered.

"They seem to have been watering a lot lately" she said in one of her slightly joking ways.

"Do you still love me?" I managed to ask.

"Oh, darling — did you think I stopped loving you when I had the baby?"

That, of course, was the case. I really did think that. She always adored tiny babies — in fact I think she enjoyed us all most when we were very small. And I was the first, and a daughter, so probably had received more attention than my siblings. Now she had another small daughter, and much less time and energy to give the rest of us than before. I felt cut off and sad.

So I myself must have become another problem for her — one that I believe could have been solved if I had ever been asked to help with Sarah, to hold her sometimes or be with her alone sometimes.

My petty jealousy of my sister lasted a long time, which was a great pity, because Sarah was a sweet little girl, always cheerful and happy. I should have been able to see that in fact I was luckier than she was. She never knew our father, and we never talked to her about him. Years later my mother's friend May told me that Sarah had asked her about her father. Sarah never asked me or the boys, and it wasn't until we were really grown up that we became fast friends.

Books were my salvation, even more than walks with my grandfather and lessons with Miss Cuddeford. I remember little about this time. What is clear, so that I can still see the scenes described in it, is the book "Bevis", by Richard Jefferies.

It was an old book, in every sense of the word. Its cover was battered, its pages muslin thin — and there were an enormous number of pages! The illustrations were pen and ink drawings, old fashioned pictures of two boys and their activities. Jefferies was a Victorian naturalist, growing up on a farm in Wiltshire. "Bevis" was based on this childhood.

Bevis and his friend Mark were more like me than anyone else I had met or even read about, especially Bevis. He was an organizer — he had great plans that didn't always work out. He was always looking for adventure — building rafts that rarely floated, sailing on the little lake near the farm, learning to swim, re-enacting the battles of Caesar and Pompey with his own group of friends and a gang of opponents. He got a lot of his ideas from books, and was always reading. And he often had moments of boredom and frustration, when nothing seemed to be going right.

I devoured this book. In Purbrook I couldn't try out Bevis' ideas, but later they had a huge influence on the way we played. And almost at the same time as my discovery of "Bevis" I heard Arthur Ransome's "Peter Duck" being read aloud on Children's Hour.

Ransome wrote about children who operated independently of adults, who went hiking and camping and sailing all on their own, who were always exploring. One of the leaders was a girl, who was as tough

73

as any boy. As soon as I could get hold of one of his books I was addicted. In the next few years I collected all of them, and still have them. They gave me more pleasure, and more ideas, than anything I've since read. They created a perfect escape, but not really from reality — they were not fantasy, they were about things that one day I would be able to do. They didn't talk down to the reader, they didn't try to 'teach' — and they certainly didn't attempt to 'improve' in any way. They were just what I needed, and I had learnt to read at just the right time.

That Christmas, 1940, brought another book — which is the only thing I remember about it. There was a big, heavy parcel from my father, wrapped in brown paper and tied up with string. How did he manage to send it from his ship, I wondered? It contained an enormous volume, bound in green cloth and very grown up looking, an anthology containing stories from every era — Greek legends, gloomy Nordic myths, Victorian morality tales, Grimm, Hans Anderson, extracts from Dickens and Stevenson and Kipling. There was enough to last me for months and suit my every mood. It led me into other worlds, and I read it for years.

We did learn something about our father's Christmas on board the Bonaventure. He had sent us a program for the Church Service on board ship, which was somewhere on the Bay of Biscay at the time. We imagined that Christmas Day. The Marine band would have been playing, the deck cold and wet. They would have sung familiar carols — "God Rest You, Merry Gentlemen" — and of course, the sailors' hymn " "Eternal father, strong to save, Whose arm doth calm the restless wave." It seemed reassuring to us all.

But much, much later I discovered that the Bonaventure had in fact been involved in its first battle that day, and probably hadn't had its service at all. It was damaged, but not severely. It was just as well we didn't know.

So the war had come to us not only in the form of sirens and bombs and sleepless nights, but in the form of very different lives, despite the familiar house, our daily routine, our mother's care. No matter how hard she tried, however much she tried to keep things normal, she was not as she'd been before, so nothing could be the same for us. Like the children in the books, I tried to live a more separate life. But my escape was mostly through those books.

74

The Letter

That winter was a blur. But I know that the bombing, which had ceased for a while after Christmas, started again as spring approached, and we went back to the cellar at nights.

Mrs. Beets had left when Sarah was about three weeks old. But later a new lady had come to live with us. Her name was Mrs. Hastelow, and she was divorced. I knew because I heard my mother asking her if she was a widow, and she said no, she was a divorcee. She was wearing a knit woolen suit, and looked round and comforting. We all liked her, and didn't even mind if she bathed us and did some of the things my mother used to do with us. She introduced us to a bathtub game that I've played with my children and grandchildren — splashing the walls by the tub, choosing a drip and seeing which one won. She didn't call my mother 'Madam' like Checkers did, and anyone else who had worked in our house. She just called her Mrs. Hayter, like most other people.

Sometime my father must have come home to see Sarah, and of course all of us. He had knitted little woolen vests for her while he was on the ship to keep himself occupied when things were quiet. But I know now that the Bonaventure had been involved in several engagements. In January it was deployed to the Mediterranean.

When he left on that one visit I remember it was evening and we were all in the drawing room. As he went out the front door and into the dark I remember thinking "Now I will write him a letter", and realizing that although he was almost within reach still, he had gone, and was as far away as if he was on the ship. How strange that seemed. It was a thought that recurred whenever I said goodbye to my children, as one by one, they went off on their travels, and I could see them on the other side of a barrier or through a window, so near, and yet already far away.

And then — as I remember this time — it happened — the day when our lives changed forever.

A pretty, sunny April morning, April 8, 1941. We're all in bed with my mother, the bright light streaming in. There's a tractor plowing the field opposite, the sound advancing and retreating as the plowman turns at our end of the field.

I'm cuddled up next to my mother, who is breast feeding baby Sarah. We're wide awake — for once we didn't have to go down to the cellar. There were no air raids last night.

And I'm happy, because it's the day before my eighth birthday. Tomorrow there'll be presents for me, here in my mother's bed. And in the afternoon there'll be a birthday party. I wonder if there'll be a present from my father, even though he's far away on his new ship Bonaventure. He always sends me presents, and writes me letters with funny drawings on them.

There's a small thud downstairs as the mail falls from our letterbox. I can hear our housekeeper, Mrs. Hastelow, getting up from the chair where she's probably drinking her early morning cup of tea. In a moment she's thumping up the stairs. "Lots of post today!" she says as she hands the letters to my mother. "And lots from John!" my mother says, her voice happy. She sorts the letters — the blue airmail letters from my father, saved to be read later, and the ordinary ones. Often several of his letters arrive all at once. She says it's because they only get picked up from the ship occasionally. Once they were all stained with sea water, and smelt. Perhaps the mail bag had fallen in.

Today she chooses a brown paper envelope. I know the most boring letters always look like that — they're official. They're just business letters. We get a lot — mostly bills, she says.

But this one is different. The letters on top say "On his Majesty's Service." She tears it open, and starts to read. Then she leans forwards and her hands go up over her face. She's shaking — I can feel her.

"What's the matter?" Mrs. Hastelow cries. My mother stretches out one hand, the letter in it. The letter is fluttering. Mrs. Hastelow reads it. "Oh, my dear!" she says. I cry — I don't know why — but I'm frightened. I snuggle up to my mother. "Why are you crying, darling?" she says in a funny, high voice, not like her normal voice. "You don't know what's happened. I'll tell you after your birthday.."

Mrs. Hastelow hustles us out of the room — all except Sarah, of course. "Get dressed, children" she says "And just leave your mother alone". She goes back in my mother's bedroom. We don't know what to do. We don't talk — until we hear my mother come out of her room and go into the bathroom. Then Howard goes to the door and calls "Shall I write to Daddy today?" There is silence a moment, then my mother says, in that same high voice, "Not today, darling" and I know why Howard asked, when he hates writing letters. And I know that something awful has happened to our father. And I don't dare ask what.

My grandparents come over, and I go for a walk with Grandpa. "You're very quiet" he says. I know he wants me to tell him why, but I can't. Perhaps I'm wrong — I hope I'm wrong. But he's quiet too. He looks as if he's been crying, but grown ups don't cry, do they?.

And then my brothers and I go over to some neighbors, and they take us to the woods to pick primroses, and then we have tea at their house, and someone asks "And where is your father now, Susan?" and I say, being grown up, " He's in the Middle East, I think", even though I don't really know where the Middle East is. And the neighbor says "Of course, you can't really know where he is — we don't want to let the Germans know, do we?" and I want to tell her what happened that day, but I know I'm not meant to. So when we get home I go out to the orchard and walk along the fence between us and next door and sing about my father, and hope someone will hear, but they don't.

The next day is my birthday. Once again we're in bed with my mother, as soon as we wake up in the morning. There are presents to unwrap, and one is from my father. It's a real, grown up painting set, beautiful brushes and little tubes of watercolors, all in a black metal case. It's just what I wanted. So perhaps I'm wrong about what happened. He did send me a present.

I look at my mother — she's looking away. And her voice is like yesterday. But I love the paint box all the same. Painting is my favorite thing.

So I paint all morning, while my brothers play with their trains. Nobody bothers us. And in the afternoon we have my party. My mother still hasn't told me anything, but my birthday isn't over yet. We do everything we usually do — we play games, like "Oranges and Lemons" and Musical Chairs, and have a Treasure Hunt, and drink lemonade and eat little bowls of pink jelly, and I blow out the candles on my birthday cake, and my mother's voice is still high and strange, and I wish I wasn't having a birthday party.

She doesn't tell me what happened, that day or the next, or the one after, and I get scared to ask. Perhaps I don't really want to know. We don't talk much — not even me and Howard and Richard. But at nights, when we used to say "God bless dear Daddy" we don't do that, and she doesn't sing us funny songs like she used to. So I tell God to bless Daddy anyway, and ask him one hundred times to let my father come home. "Perhaps they divorced?" I ask Howard one day, but we don't know much about divorce. Only Uncle Jimmy and Mrs. Hastelow did that, and we still see them.

Once I dream that my father comes home. It's the only time I do. It's a lovely dream, until I wake up and remember.

And the bombing starts again, and we spend our nights in the cellar. And one night there's a really loud roar, and the house shakes a lot, and my mother says "That's us!" and she jumps up and runs up the stairs, and so does Mrs. Hastelow. So Howard and Richard and I run up too — the baby is left behind in her carry cot. We look out the kitchen door. It's all bright outside — there's a huge fire blazing underneath the clothes line that had Sarah's diapers on it — except those diapers aren't there any more. "I'll get the sand bag" my mother says. "No you don't!" says Mrs. Hastelow. She picks up the heavy sand bag outside the door and runs out to dump it on the fire. She runs back in. "An incendiary bomb, I expect" she says. Then we go back to the cellar. And next day there's a great big black ring, like when we've had a bonfire, only much bigger, and it's still hot.

I get in trouble one day. We don't go exploring in the woods any more, so I take the boys for a walk along the big road, where we're not meant to go. We don't go far, but soon my mother comes up behind us, and she's very cross with me. I know it's my fault.

I read a lot. I read nearly all the big book my father gave me for Christmas. But I don't read the sad, gloomy ones — the ones about people who die, people who get killed.

Sometimes I go into the tiny lobby by the front door. My father's camel hair coat is hanging there, waiting for him to come home. I bury my nose in it. The soft beige wool smells like him — his tobacco, his 4711 cologne.

One morning we're having breakfast, sitting at the old wood table in our green painted kitchen. I remember my mother painting it green. My grandmother was there, and she said green was an unlucky color. I wondered why, when green is the color of nice things like trees and grass. But perhaps it really is. Mum says "There's something I want to talk to you about". I feel fluttery. Will she tell us about our father? But she says "Would you like to go and stay with Grandma and Grandpa in Devon?".

We don't know what to say. She's never asked us to decide anything before. I wonder what she wants us to say. We went to Devon last summer, and I didn't want to come home — I liked it so much. But our mother doesn't like Grandma too much. And do I really want to leave our new tabby kitten, Kit, and our Grandma and Grandpa here? And our house, with the orchard, and our swing on the walnut tree? And what happens if Daddy comes back and we're not here? But I don't say that. We don't say anything.

And then one day there's a taxi outside to take us to Devon. We say goodbye to Mrs. Hastelow, and Kit. We put Sarah, in her blue carry cot, on the floor in the back of the taxi. Our mother sits in front with the taxi driver. It's a long drive, and I go to sleep some of the time. When I wake up my mother says "You missed a very old house we passed" and I'm sorry, because I love old houses, and castles. And the journey begins to be a bit exciting, especially when we go down the lane where our grandparents live, and it's so narrow the flowers on the banks on each side come in through the open windows, and it smells all country-ish, and lovely. And there are our grandparents coming down the drive to meet us and hug us, and we're there at last.

That Summer with Our Grandparents

Our grandparents' little house seemed like heaven, with the fields and woods behind it and the beautiful view of the cliffs and hills in the front. It was so quiet — no traffic, and no planes overhead — except, amazingly, on our second night there, when the siren sounded and we heard the familiar sound of a bomb whistling down — but no explosion! The wheat was coming up, and the bomb fell in its midst and wasn't discovered until months later — but that's another story. We forgot about it.

In the mornings we were wakened by the birds and the boy in the nearby farm calling the cows in for milking, and in the evenings we'd hear him again.

The house was familiar. In the living room we remembered the pictures on the walls, mostly watercolors by Great Aunt Emmie, the big wooden musical box that Richard loved, and the cabinet with a glass front and inside, rows of little Chinamen with nodding heads. It felt like home. But Howard was sad. When we sat down to tea that first day he wanted to sit next to my mother, so I knew. Richard just wanted to hear the music box. But although my grandparents must have been full of grief I noticed nothing. My father had been their oldest child, and a special one — the one everyone loved and looked up to. But nobody talked about him, and I know I didn't. I was so happy to be there.

I loved Grandma and Grandpa Hayter. Even though I hadn't spent much time with them I felt perfectly at home there. The big thing was that they talked to me as a person, not just as a little girl. And like all the Wakefields, Grandma's family, they hugged each other a lot, talked and argued and teased each other. They seemed more easy going, relaxed, than my mother's family. It seems to me that growing up in India, and perhaps having Indian blood, made them different from people who had been born and brought up in Britain. They didn't have so many rules, they ate different things, they didn't mind if we stayed up late or forgot to come in for lunch. And I loved Grandma's cooking! She made curries and chapattis and dhal, and Scotch eggs and Gooseberry Fool and other unfamiliar but delicious things. They were quite different from our usual very plain food, tastier, probably influenced by her Indian background. And she actually liked having me in the kitchen with her and talking to me while she cooked. I felt close to her, and special.

She found out what I liked to eat, and tried to make it. Sometimes her efforts weren't successful — like when she tried to make lemon curd. Real lemons had disappeared early on in the war, so she used lemon essence, and it tasted awful. Then she was a little hurt because we didn't like it. Another thing we didn't like was her milk. She boiled all milk, as they had had to do in India, and stored it in the fridge. We had all hated hot milk, and this was just as bad. We wouldn't drink it!

Grandma's house had all the equipment ours didn't. There was a large refrigerator, a Hoover vacuum cleaner, and a primitive toaster. The toaster's grill was in its center, in a vertical position, and on each side there were flaps which came down so that you could put the bread in, then you closed it up. But you had to watch it, because it didn't stop until you took the toast out, and one of my main memories of that house is the smell of burnt toast. Grandma, like most women, was a multi tasker, and would always be frying the eggs or making the tea while the bread was toasting, until suddenly there would be a cry of distress, and the charred objects had to be removed from the toaster. We children were often delegated to watch the toasting progress.

There was no doubt who ruled the house. It was definitely Grandma — strong, opinionated, full of inventive schemes and plans. Our grandfather, 'Tubs' as she called him, was a kind, gentle and rather remote figure, disappearing into his little cluttered study by the front door with his books about India, his writing materials, his cigarettes — they both smoked heavily. Outside his door was a framed Hayter family tree, which he sometimes used to identify strange relatives for us. In time we would know many of them. We weren't allowed into his study, but that was fine. We were used to being kept to certain parts of the house, and in this one we were actually much freer than we'd been before.

The garden itself had attractions — it was bigger than ours had been, with an extensive lawn, and several rather untidy flower beds.

Grandpa dug these, Grandma looked after them, but wasn't too fussy about picking up weeds or cutting back overgrown shrubs. My mother complained to us about that — she didn't like gardening, but did it to keep things tidy. Her flower beds were always neat.

On one side of the lawn there was a little garden shed. It had windows and a little porch, and was meant for us. Inside it smelt deliciously of cedar wood. And in it was a large rocking horse, with a mane and tail and real looking reins and saddle. The hut was big enough to play in, or even sleep in, which we never did. I would have felt scared in the dark.

On the other side of the lawn a bank separated us from the grounds of a large, sprawling red brick house which was a girls' 'prep school'. We would climb up on the bank and watch the girls at recess, or exercising on their outside gym. I longed to be one of them — and in fact I was soon told that I'd be going there in September.

We could go out through the back garden, past the fenced enclosure where Grandma kept her chickens– Rhode Island Reds and White Leghorns, she called them — and on into the field behind. We had to walk round the edge of the field because that was where the wheat was growing — and the bomb was hidden! But we didn't know that. Then there was a bank, topped by a hedge. But the hedge wasn't too dense, and we could get through into a meadow that sloped downhill to a little stream. There were often cows in the meadow, big dark red cows, but we were used to cows — we knew they usually ran away from us — and we went on, jumping across the stream where it was narrowest. All around the stream the ground was churned up by the cows, forming little hillocks, so we'd often get pretty muddy and damp. Then up the hill on the other side, up to a pine wood, where the ground was smooth and slippery with pine needles, and the bare trunks soared up around us to the branches far above. If there was a breeze there was a beautiful sighing sound. It was a lovely peaceful place to be, quite different from the deciduous woods around Purbrook, with their undergrowth and fallen logs.

Nobody seemed to worry about our wanderings. I was free to start exploring as Bevis or the Arthur Ransome children had done. I began to forget the war.

It was late May when we arrived, and the banks along the narrow lanes were covered in wild flowers. I wanted to know their names. Grandma took me down to the local bookshop, and we found a book about flowers. My father had found me the same sort of book when I wanted to know the names of birds. So I can still name those flowers — Ragged Robin, Scabious, Jack in the Pulpit, Pimpernel, Red Campion, Foxglove, Cow Parsley, Queen Anne's Lace — many more. There were still Cowslips, taller yellow relatives of Primroses. The primroses and bluebells were almost over when we arrived, but in the meadows opposite the house we found a valley that had been covered with them earlier on. We named it "Primrose Valley" and every year thereafter we visited it in the springtime.

Grandma loved flowers too, and tried growing unusual plants in her garden. So there for the first time I saw yellow bush lupines, just the same plants as grow wild in the hills of Northern California where I live now, and real American corn. So I ate corn there for the first time. I didn't taste it again until my husband and I emigrated to Canada seventeen years later.

Together Grandma and I went shopping for my own small patch of garden. In the village shop we found packages of seeds. I chose California Poppies.

"They'll take over the garden!" Grandma told me, but she let me buy them anyway — and they did.

She took me to a café on the High Street that ran parallel to the beach; we had tea and cakes, and afterwards I saw a beautiful hat — a straw hat with flowers around the brim. I longed for it, and she bought it for me. But that didn't turn out so well — as I have said, my mother didn't approve of hats on children and made her take it back.

It's quite likely that my mother felt that I was getting more attention than Howard and Richard — and it's possible that I was. With my mother's determination that we should all be treated alike this would not have gone down well, and may have increased the mistrust that she felt for my grandmother. They were two grieving women in a very small house, with totally different experiences in life and attitudes towards bringing up children. There was almost bound to be trouble.

We found our mother one day in her tiny attic bedroom. She was crying, with letters from our father all over the bed. We'd never seen her cry. "It's all right, chicks" she said "It's just my eyes watering." We crept downstairs, silent, helpless.

Another brown letter came, addressed to 'The Execution of J.O.G. Hayter'. Surely he hadn't been beheaded? But nobody told us anything, and one day I heard my grandmother say to my mother. "So it's still 'Let sleeping dogs lie?'" and I knew what that meant, and I knew she meant us. We were the dogs.

Later, while I was riding the rocking horse on the parched summer lawn, Grandma asked me "Do you remember your father?" I was angry, too angry to be polite. "Of course I do!" I yelled. And she never mentioned him again.

So Howard and I needed to talk. We had nobody else to talk with about our father and our questions. One day, on a walk down to town, we hid behind a bush in the small grassy park. We came up with an answer., but we didn't know if it was right. We had seen pictures of ships going down, sailors sliding down slanting decks. I tried not to look, but I had to. Our father was a marine, not a sailor, but he was on a ship.

And perhaps my mother really needed to talk too. One beautiful, golden evening She took me for a walk along a lane called Kersbrook, on a ridge above a little valley full of farms and cows and green fields. There was honeysuckle in the hedges, smelling wonderful. I pulled out petals and sucked the nectar — my grandmother had shown me how. I could feel my mother wanted to tell me something. She seemed nervous, so I was too. But she couldn't manage it. Our walk ended mostly in silence.

Howard was even more attuned to our mother's moods than I was — he worried a lot, and probably missed our home in Purbrook more. The relatives all called him "little man" and told him how he needed to look after his mother — even if they did not tell him why. But what could a six year old do about his worries? We were both alone with our own thoughts, but I had more to occupy me — my books, my painting, the countryside, the newly discovered relatives.

But there was so much to do and explore. We were used to our father being away and didn't think of him all the time We wanted our mother to be as she had been, but apart from our daily walks we saw less of her than we ever had. She was busy with Sarah, and beyond that we were on our own, or with one of our grandparents. For me, the freedom, and the beauty of the countryside were consoling.

This could have been — should have been — a time when we mourned our father, gathered as a family to comfort each other. Looking back, I think my grandmother understood our distress, and I think she also found the countryside consoling.

Petrol was not yet rationed, and every so often she would pack us all up in the little Morris Oxford and our grandfather would drive us off for a picnic. The places she chose were a bit unusual. There was an abandoned orchard, filled with the continual thrumming of an ancient watermill. I discovered it on my own, dark and forbidding, eerie — scary. I fled from it, back to the sunlit safety of the orchard, the familiar blanket spread on the grass, the ham sandwiches and Scotch eggs, the 'Lemon Squash" in a thermos flask, the Bakelight mugs, the loved voices.

Another faintly haunted place was a ruined mansion on the hills above Exmouth, surrounded by dark overgrown rhododendrons and azaleas with winding paths between them. It was too easy to imagine fierce animals hiding in wait behind the bushes. I did not really like Grandma's choices.

But perhaps these places reminded Grandma of the ruins found in the jungles of India, where the whole family would accompany our grandfather on tours of his district. The servants would set up the camp, being careful to fix a clothes line between two trees for the latest baby's diapers. The children would play in the forest, and our grandparents, both of them, would take their rifles and go off to shoot game for dinner. Both were very good shots. They must have missed those earlier days with their children.

Later on my grandfather sometimes broke the law in Budleigh by shooting pheasants and rabbits from their living room windows. These became a very useful part of our diet when food was strictly rationed. And my grandfather would take his rifle with him when he went off to train in the Home Guard. Most of the men, all elderly, didn't have guns, and marched with heavy wooden poles instead.

It never occurred to us that our grandparents must have been feeling as sad, or sadder, than we were. They both, perhaps, looked into the past for comfort. I have no idea if we were any comfort at all.

Just occasionally our grandfather too would take us for a walk. He was full of knowledge about the area — knew the dates of the ancient churches, could tell you wherever a muddy lane might lead, and could tell you the history of most of the old cottages and farms around us. Once he took me to Hayes Barton, the large farmhouse where Sir Walter Raleigh was born. It was a long walk across fields, through woods and along little lanes. The house was a thatched farmhouse built in the shape of an E, to honor Queen Elizabeth, and was then open to the public, though still a working farm. We went inside, seeing a letter written by Raleigh, the kitchen with its high oak settles beside the huge black fireplace. I knew about Raleigh, but it was my grandfather who told me why the settles were built that way, and the way the spit in the fireplace worked.

It was during that summer, so happy in many ways, that both Howard and I became constantly aware of our elders' feelings, especially our mother's. Much as I loved our grandparents, I did not feel free to show it, and we were constantly trying to please our mother. Once, when she offered to cook dinner, we were delighted — it was a chance for her to show what a good cook she was, and (we hoped) feel better. She made a rabbit stew, which we usually liked, but it didn't turn out quite right. She was disappointed, and we were sad for her.

So it was a summer of dichotomy, of happiness at being away from the bombing, at being in a beautiful place where we were free to explore, and being with grandparents we loved — but with the constant sadness around our mother and the silence about the person we wanted most to talk about.

Budleigh Relatives

Sometimes we heard our grandmother talking on the phone in a different language. We knew who she was talking to — it was one of her sisters, Aunt Ivy or Aunt Una. Each of them also lived in Budleigh — had done in fact for much longer than our grandparents. They were the reason my grandparents had moved to Budleigh. And the reason they spoke Hindustani to each other was that they had grown up speaking that Anglicised version of Hindi when they were children in India. It was what their 'Ayah' spoke to them, and what they spoke to the servants.

There was probably another reason –that they could speak privately because neither we nor our mother could understand it. It can't have helped our mother feel at home, though she liked both her aunts in law and found them easier to get on with than her mother in law. Our grandmother was very close to her sisters. They and their husbands often came over to play bridge — long, argumentative games, when they took over the living room and didn't take any notice of us. My mother played bridge too, but never joined this group. She said they played a different sort of bridge.

But we did often walk around to visit each of them, and became very fond of them, especially Aunt Ivy. She was slim and elegant, with the family's smudged dark eyes and high cheek bones. Her husband, Uncle Lovelace Carter, was the opposite. He was short and squat, with a huge head. A family story was that an anthropology journal had published a photo of him as a 'perfect example of Neanderthal man'. He came from a prosperous local family who owned a large building business, but he was the family intellectual — a graduate of Peterhouse, Cambridge, and fascinated by archaeology, anthropology, science of all sorts, and music. Later he taught me almost all I knew about classical music. He collected Roman coins which he dug up in the countryside around, and had bits of early British pottery and weapons in a small 'museum' up on the cliffs.

He was also mentioned in Max Perutz's Nobel Prize winner's speech — for his discovery of radio-active nodules in the cliffs of Budleigh.

And even though his early childhood had been spent in India, and his ancestors had been there as long as the Wakefields, his was an old Devon family, and he too loved his familiar countryside. Years and years later, when I was an undergraduate and spent a week with them, he took me to see his 'private park', a view across a five barred gate to an expansive stretch of green pastureland rising up to the gold and purple of Woodbury Common. He liked just to sit and look at it.

Aunt Ivy was the one who had taught my father and his siblings to read as children in India, before they were left in Scotland to go to school. All of them later said that they were far ahead in reading and writing, History and Geography when they eventually went to school in Scotland, but were woefully behind in Math! She had made a 'good' marriage — in fact all her sisters did too, despite being part Indian. They were all beautiful and talented. Uncle Lovelace was a lawyer in the Indian Civil Service, the 'elite' of the British administration. Like all the sisters, Aunt Ivy had never done housework or cooking until she came to England. But like them, she was inventive and pioneering in her domestic activities. She made elderberry wine and rhubarb wine, curries and wonderful soups, and wasn't a compulsive housewife.

I loved Pine Hollow, their house, a fairly large Edwardian built on the steep slope that led up to the cliff tops. You could go through a gate behind the house and climb up through some pine woods then onto a wide grassy area on the cliffs where we could play 'French cricket' — there were always old cricket bats and wickets stored under the stairs in the hall.

The house was surrounded by a beautiful garden, with a grass tennis court immediately in front of it. Beside that were topiary animals, and a cedar hut like an older version of ours, and below it vegetable gardens, and a grassy area designed to be an outdoor theater for the Carter children when they put on their plays. There were four of them, John, Mary, Marjorie and Ruth. Once, several years before, we'd been there for a performance of "Snow White" in full costume, with elaborate scenery. We'd been entranced by these glamorous, accomplished older cousins — they were probably all in their late teens or early twenties then. The cedar hut had been John's special place. He had pasted cuttings from old magazines on the walls — photos of the Royal family, and early film stars, and trains and old fashioned cars.

Now these children were all grown up, and away from home — John in the army, the girls at University or in jobs. But it was still a garden meant for children — rolling down the bank onto the tennis court, playing house in the hut, or hide and seek among all the shrubs.

And inside had its attractions too — not just Uncle Lovelace's collections, but a large gray parrot who lived in a cage in the kitchen. It had come back from India with them in the 20s. Polly greeted one with a hoarse "Hello, hello"! then followed throughout the visit with very parrot-ish remarks — nothing very original, but fascinating to us, who had never seen a talking bird.

Polly died at a ripe old age, but the rest of the kitchen has remained the same to this day. A large oak table in the middle, glass fronted cabinets filled with Crown Derby china, a linoleum floor, a door into the scullery where the actual cooking was done. Aunt Ivy was careful to keep to the rules presumably set by our mother — only rarely did she forget and mention our father. Once she told us how he would be sent to his room if he didn't eat his porridge for breakfast, and it would be served to him at every meal until he finished it. "He was such a sweet little boy!" she sighed. She had obviously felt that our grandmother was unnecessarily strict. It gave us a different view of her — and it also gave us a glimpse of our father as a child. He was older by the time the Carters had moved into Pine Hollow, but he must have been there many times, and it was nice to think of that. It had been a base for many of the Wakefield cousins coming back from India, and it was still a house that welcomed guests.

One of those visiting cousins, Colonel John Wakefield, stayed on in India after independence, and founded a chain of 'jungle lodges' in wilder areas of India. Brian and I stayed at one near Mysore, Kabini River Lodge on the edge of Nagarhole National Park, when we were there in 2004; he was ninety then and living at the lodge, but he was away at a 'tiger camp' in Nepal. Like so many one time tiger hunters he had become a conservationist. and very active in the movement to preserve India's wildlife. I talked to him on his cell phone as he sat by the fire in camp — he remembered me as a baby in England, but most of all he remembered Pine Hollow.

My other Budleigh great aunt was Aunt Una. She was the youngest of the three, short, plump, and out going — that is, with family.
Otherwise she was somewhat of a recluse. Her husband, Uncle Ken,
was very quiet, but kind and friendly. He had been an engineer in India.
They lived in a tall Victorian semi detached house on our way down
to Budleigh, and had a shaded, rather gloomy living room filled with
ancient Indian furniture and animal rugs, with large, pallid watercolors
of maritime scenes on the walls. They too had a glass fronted cabinet,
and once Aunt Una took a little glass vial out of it, opened the top and
made me sniff the contents.

"That, Susan, is the smell of India!" she announced. I was not impressed. The contents, whatever they were, had lost their scent in the
last twenty years. But I couldn't tell Aunt Una that. It obviously meant
a lot to her to have me experience something of her beloved India.

They had a son, Ian, who replaced Peter in my affections for a
while. He must have been older, perhaps thirteen at the time. He had
a bike, a large room filled with trains and microscopes and all sorts of
games and sports equipment. I admired him enormously, and I think he
enjoyed that. He was my father's youngest cousin. Aunt Una seemed
so old to me that it seemed strange that she had a son who played with
me — but he too was very shy with most people, and only seemed
comfortable with us or the Carters. Unfortunately I became shy and self
conscious with him as a result of the English habit of teasing children.
My grandmother very briefly had a maid, who took all of us children
for a walk in the fields one day. We were playing a game that involved
using buttercups to answer questions. You had to hold the flower under
your chin, and if it reflected you had to answer a question. This maid
asked if I liked Ian. "I love him!" I declared. That meant endless teasing
from all the adults, so much so that I hardly dared to talk to Ian again.

We all teased each other, and the adults teased us. I thought myself
ugly for years, because my brothers were always commenting on my
large nose — and I'm sure I did the same to them. It was often painful,
and had lasting effect.

I loved having all these interesting relatives around. They seemed
to like us too, and they were certainly one of the reasons I felt so at
home in Budleigh.

Moving Again

O ne day my mother gathered us around her once more. She told us that the bombing seemed to have stopped in Portsmouth, and asked if we would like to go home. The problem was that we — or certainly I — no longer thought of Purbrook as 'home'. This was home, with our grandparents and other family around us, and the beautiful countryside to explore. This time I had no hesitation about answering — I did not think for one moment about what my mother wanted. "No!" I said.

I have no idea if that swayed her in her decision. Perhaps she herself was not ready to go back to the Portsmouth area, with all its memories and associations. Once, before we left, she had gone down to Portsmouth center, and had come back saying she didn't even know where she was. This was the town where she had grown up, and knew every street, every building. Handleys, the department store where we'd gone for tea and to look at the toy shop, was completely gone; so was most of the Guildhall — so were the places she'd danced and partied with my father.

I think, too, that my grandparents must have offered to help her buy a house. Even if the occasional air raid dropped a bomb or two on Budleigh, which did happen, it was nothing like Portsmouth, and she could see how happy we were. In any case, she started to house hunt, and this seemed to bring her to life again. She and my father had never owned a house. Even Rosyth had been rented, and we had only lived there for three years, though it seemed an age to me. So there must have been some excitement in the idea of owning her own home. We went with her to other parts of Budleigh, touring dark, neglected interiors and cheerful, light filled houses, terrace houses and cottages and big houses with beautiful furniture.

Once we looked at a lovely house with the attractive name "Swift Arrow". It was perched on a small hill overlooking the estuary of the little River Otter and the steep shingle bank beyond that protected the marshland from the sea. There was a wide green lawn, and views from every window. My mother loved it, and so did we. "Let's buy this one!" we pleaded. But it was too expensive, and we started to look in less exclusive areas. That meant going by bus, first to the little town called Topsham on the River Exe, where we saw a house we also loved, an old red brick Georgian with a walled garden behind it, and fruit trees growing up the walls. But that also cost much too much. Finally she found the house that became our home for the next eight years, a semi detached house on a quiet street in Exmouth, the closest town to Budleigh. It was right on the edge of town, and there were just the houses opposite between us and the open fields.

During this house hunting time we met someone who became one of the most important people in our lives. She arrived one day with our aunt Georgie, who had still kept up her visits to us on her time off from nursing. Georgie would stay just up the lane from Furzebank, our grandparents' house, at a house that did bed and breakfast. Villagers often did that in a casual, unregulated way in those days.

This time a young girl came with her. We met her on the lane; she was quite tall, curly haired, with a pretty though acne scarred face, and turned out to be just sixteen years old. We liked her from the start, though she was very shy — so shy that she hardly dared to talk to the grown ups. But she talked to us children — and talked in the way we liked, listening to us, treating us as real people.

Her name was Joyce Kinge, with the G pronounced like a J. She came to be looked over as a 'home help' for my mother. Georgie had been living in a nurses' home, a large mansion that had been taken over for that purpose at the beginning of the war. The housekeeper there had been Joyce's mother; her father was gardener for the grounds. There were two sisters, one of whom was bound for college; the other had a good civil service job.

Of course we children didn't know anything of all this then, but apparently Joyce had been a problem — not in any unpleasant way, but because she was so abnormally shy — shy in a paralyzing way, that had made school and later on a job impossible for her. She had left school at the routine leaving age of fourteen, gone into 'service' with some family, and had simply been unable to function. Georgie had become very fond of her parents, and had learnt how desperate they were about Joyce. She was too young to be called up for war work, and there didn't seem to be many opportunities for her.

So even though she didn't, on the face of it, look an ideal prospect as a help for a young widow with four small children, my mother took her on. She always got on well with teenagers (though not so much with me later on!) and she doubtless felt sorry for Joyce.

I had already heard of her, because she had made beautiful clothes for two dolls Georgie had bought for me — clothes Joyce had designed herself and sewn by hand with tiny, perfect stitches. They were the most elegant dolls I had ever had. I wasn't particularly fond of them, because I really only liked realistic baby dolls, but I admired them tremendously. She had also brought, on her visit to Budleigh, a dress she had made for me. It was sleeveless, and had a floral pattern that included black. I had never had a dress with black in it, and thought it very sophisticated. And even though it wasn't what my mother would have chosen for me, I was allowed to wear it.

So Joyce had created a favorable impression at least on me. But she must have appealed to my mother too. I expect she responded well to my mother, who was good at making people feel at home and comfortable. For our mother, the activity of house hunting and quite probably the prospect of having help in the house and with us seemed to bring her back to life a little.. And Joyce became a blessing. She went back with Georgie that time, but as soon as we moved into our new home she was there.

The Background Shadow

In Portsmouth the war had been in the forefront of our minds. Now it was retreating further back, but there was never a moment when we were not aware of it. It might be as our grandfather went off to his 'Home Guard' duty, with his rifle strapped to his back. It might be as we walked down to the town, and passed a house with a crater to one side of it, and its wall partly gone, the windows blown in. On the beach there were concrete blocks placed in the pebbles to act as hopeful barricades against invading tanks. Barbed wire covered most access to the beaches. Occasional booms signaled the accidental explosion of one of the mines planted in the Chine, a steep ravine leading down from the top of the cliffs — another possible route for invaders. On a shopping trip to Exmouth with Grandma, chiefly to buy some more doll clothes, we found the little street housing the toy shop mostly destroyed, shattered walls and windows, roofless buildings — though luckily the toy shop had survived.

There were no real military targets in these small towns — they were mostly terror attacks — an aircraft or two zooming in from the sea, dropping a few bombs, and escaping unscathed. But there were also RAF airfields nearby, and one of our favorite sounds was the whine of a Spitfire engine as a fighter sped over us to patrol out to sea. None of our adults were terrorized by these attacks, so my own fears diminished. I still prayed every night for an end to the war, after asking God for blessings on all my family, and my hundred requests that my father would come home.

There were other aspects of war that were less important to us children, but difficult for our adults. Many food items — bananas, lemons, most imported foods — had already disappeared. Rationing was strict — milk, meat, butter, sugar, eggs, jam, cheese, cooking fats, tea, coffee, — were only available in tiny quantities. 'Luxury' foods, like icing sugar for our birthday cakes, became almost unobtainable. There were special allowances for babies and children — orange juice, extra milk. We all had ration books, geared to our circumstances, and in fact the overall health of the British population improved during the war, due to price controls and the emphasis of the rationing system on healthy foods. Vegetables were not rationed, and our grandmother grew many of them in her own garden.

All of this demanded a lot of ingenuity in planning meals and producing them. But those weren't the only things rationed. I distinctly remember hearing the announcement on clothes rationing on the radio. That was when we were still at our grandparents', so it was in 1941. Clothing rationing extended to shoes, buttons, all fabrics, and household textiles. Frills and lace were banned, pleats buttons and pockets restricted.

My grandparents were philosophical about this, and I didn't take much notice of it, but it certainly affected our lives later on. When my feet started growing fast, and my shoes became agonizingly tight, my mother couldn't always buy me new ones. Partly this may have been because she was perpetually short of money, but the other thing was that you were only allowed enough clothing coupons for one or two pairs of shoes a year. I remember trying to pull my tight leather shoes on over my chilblain swollen toes — it hurt so much, but there was no point in complaining about it.

Gas rationing affected us too, though our little family never had a car. But my grandfather's car, always known as Eggy, because of its number plate, had to be put up on blocks in the garage till after the end of the war — gasoline was rationed too, and most private car use was banned. We were used to walking and using buses, but there were no more trips in Eggy to deserted orchards or ruined mansions.

And soap was rationed too, and all heating fuel, and so was paper. I used to run out of paper to draw or write on, so I'd cut the end pages out of my books and use them for my artistic endeavors.

There were so many effects and implications of rationing — and at the age of eight most of it didn't matter too much to me. It was much more difficult for our elders. But all of us simply accepted things as they were. For us children it was all going on over our heads. Things might be different, but they weren't so different after all.

We often heard the adults talking nostalgically about 'before the war' — or even, in the case of the older ones, comparing it with 'the last war'. For them, the jump from a fairly comfortable, secure life must have been traumatic. They didn't grumble — they observed the rules — but they didn't go in for patriotic gestures or statements. They did what they had to do cheerfully and without drama of any sort.

Many people, when invited out to tea, would take along a jar of milk so that their hostess wouldn't have to use her rations. It seemed a reasonable enough gesture to me, then and now, but my mother, determined to behave as if war wasn't going to make any difference in her life, always insisted that her guests should not do that. In fact she was probably right; milk was one thing we always seemed to have enough of. But then, unlike most children, we didn't drink much milk. We drank water — and I suppose we got enough calcium from all the green vegetables we ate to keep us healthy and give us strong bones, because we were all amazingly free from illnesses of any sort, and were certainly tough and strong. Our diet, in fact, now strongly resembles that recommended for the American population, and as well as that we got more than enough exercise because we played outside most of the time we were home, had sports every day at school for most of the afternoon, and walked or rode bikes almost everywhere we went.

We certainly often felt hungry, but bread, at least, was not rationed, and nor was fruit. And it was all cheap because of price controls. One could always fill up on something, though there was no such thing as raiding the refrigerator, even if we'd had one — not under my mother's rule!

School

The big event of that autumn, before we moved to our house in December, was going to school for the first time. When we first arrived in Budleigh the girls had still been at school in the big red brick building next door, and I would hang on the gate and watch them going up and down the lane. Sometimes one of them would even say "hello" to me! I was really anxious to go to school. I had loved my lessons with Miss Cuddeford, and I imagined that in a real school learning would be even more interesting. Also, I'd been reading books about schoolgirls, all of them about boarding schools where students seemed to have lots of fun — they might occasionally get into trouble for what seemed to me rather minor offences, but generally it sounded exciting.

When my mother took me to look over Copplestone House School it seemed to fulfill all my expectations. It was very pretty. There was a big, sunny dormitory with two rows of beds, each covered in identical white counterpanes. I was not going to be a boarder, but many of the girls were. Then there was a big bathroom area, with shiny toilets and bathtubs and even showers, the first I'd ever seen. Some of the classrooms were in the house, others were in a large wooden building outside. There was a spacious indoor gym with climbing bars and ropes, vaulting 'horses' and balance bars — just like in the books. Outside was another gymnastics area, with the same bars and ropes. There were tennis courts and playing fields for netball and hockey. And in one corner, close to my grandparents' fence, was a lovely little chapel with light colored wooden pews and a bright blue carpet. We had heard the girls singing hymns in it. Now I'd be doing that too!

Nobody checked to see if I could actually read and write, add, subtract and divide. It was simply assumed that I would go into a class with my age group. I had missed two whole years of school.

I don't know who was going to pay for me to go to that school. I imagine it was fairly expensive, and that my grandparents helped. There was actually a 'council school' — the local public school, at the bottom of the lane, but it was never suggested that I should go there. The children there dashed around their concrete playground shrieking madly, making much more noise that we ever heard from the school next door. I never thought I would want to go there. Copplestone House School would be the start for me of a school career totally segregated from the mass of the English population, among children who all had the same accents as I did (though it wouldn't have been considered an accent, it was 'proper English'), who all had much the same backgrounds and assumptions, who all subconsciously recognized each other as familiar beings. My parents, my grandparents on both sides, were about as unsnobbish as anyone at that time, but there were unspoken rules that were automatically obeyed.

Until I left school at the age of eighteen and went to Cambridge I had never met socially anyone who came from another class. And then I was secretly surprised to find that those students who had been to State schools were just as well educated as I was — although I had suspected this all along.

At any rate, I was thrilled with my visit to Copplestone, and couldn't wait for school to start in September.

Of course I had to have a uniform. It had to be ordered from a firm in London, and I don't know how all that regulation clothing fitted in with rationing limitations. There was a beige wool sweater with a bright blue band round the neckline. That was for everyday use, and since it was still quite warm when school started it was hot and itchy to wear. Below it went a bright blue wool pleated skirt.

Under the skirt you had to wear bright blue 'puff pants' — bloomers in a cotton fabric. When we had gym or team games we took off the skirt and the sweater, donned a white short sleeved shirt, also required, and exercised in our puff pants and shirt. If we were muddy or too sweaty we might be allowed to take a shower afterwards, but mostly we just changed, sweaty or not, back into our regular uniform. We had blue blazers with the school badge on their front pockets. Then there were gray felt hats in winter, straw ones for summer, thick white sweaters for tennis — all decorated with the badge. And finally there were gym shoes, indoor shoes, out door shoes, and summer dresses, the last being bright blue cotton with white collars and cuffs.

All quite attractive, but generally uncomfortable and hard to keep clean, especially when all washing was done by hand and dry cleaning was hard to find. I hate to think what we all smelt like after a game of netball! But for me the uniform was all part of the excitement of going to school.

That excitement soon faded. The reality was not at all the glamorous picture I'd conjured up from the books I'd read and the initial visit to the school. I only had to walk next door, but the atmosphere couldn't have been more different from the warm, friendly feeling of my grandparents' home.

It began well. 'Prayers', in the cheerful little chapel, was enjoyable, and reasonably familiar, thanks to Miss Cuddeford. We sang a hymn I could still sing today —

'Jesus calls us o'er the tumult
Of our lives' tempestuous sea'.

I liked the tune, and the second verse, with its mention of St. Andrew, "by the Galilean Lake" aroused an image of a lake in Arthur Ransome's books.

But the dominant memory of my first day of school is of extreme discomfort, both physical and emotional. Perhaps somebody spoke to me. I don't remember it. Classes came and went in a blur. I had no trouble with any of them. It seemed as if my two years with Miss Cuddeford had left me better prepared than any of my classmates, especially in reading. I was shocked to find that some of them could barely read aloud — so I rapidly started a practice that continued all my school career — of reading way ahead of the teacher's instructions. We moved from room to room, about a half hour for each subject.

At some point a bell summoned us for lunch. We trooped across to the elegant dining room, with its polished wooden tables fully set with cutlery and glasses, and were told where to sit. There was a butler, clad in full morning dress — striped trousers, black jacket — who presided over the meal and watched over the serving staff. His name was Stone, someone said. I had never seen a butler before. Once seated, I had an immediate problem — I had never used a knife and fork together! In fact I had used a spoon on almost everything. I have no idea why my mother had neglected this part of our education — perhaps it was simply easier and less messy to have us continue in our baby ways — but it caused me enormous embarrassment, as I struggled to eat the horrible meal while watching my neighbors to make sure I didn't do the wrong things. Americans find it difficult to eat British style, with knife in the right hand and fork in the left, neither to be used on their own. I found it almost impossible, especially as my companions ate at breakneck speed. And the food was the worst I had ever had. That first school meal is clear in my mind — we had undercooked ground beef, known as 'mince' in Britain, boiled potatoes, and boiled cabbage.

After lunch there was singing, led by our only male teacher, Mr. Robinson. He was quite young, with blue, close shaven cheeks and chin, and he must have had something wrong with him, or he wouldn't have been teaching music to little girls instead of being off in the war. It was during this class that I realized that I finally couldn't put off going to the toilet — the 'loo' as it was called in Britain. I'd been feeling more and more desperate, but hadn't known how to ask. Another girl had asked "to be excused" so I guessed that this was the magic wording, and fortunately Mr. Robinson let me go. But I didn't know where to go. The other girl had gone to the main building, but once there I looked frantically for signs, and could see nothing. I was too shy and afraid to ask, so I walked round the traffic circle in front of the school hoping to find a sheltering bush that I could use. No such luck — so back to class I went, hoping miserably that I could hold out.

I did — through singing, through another humiliating experience, this time with netball, a game I knew nothing about — and all through the afternoon until the last class, English literature. Here I dared ask once more, and this time told the teacher I didn't know where to go. A girl was delegated to show me. Relief was finally at hand! So I got to the last class, which was just as well, because that class persuaded me that school just might be bearable. Our teacher read us the first chapter of "Wind in the Willows". The wonderful adventures of Mole and Rattty took me into another world, and my first day ended with pleasure and some hope.

Nobody expected school to be pleasant in those days, so I don't suppose anyone was surprised if I didn't seem overjoyed when I went home. I am quite sure I did not tell them — that would have been against all my instincts. I doubt if any of us three children would have expressed our feelings — we had learned by example not to do so.

It was not a bad school, probably better than most. There was much about it I learned to enjoy, and my problems were only those of any child who tended to be a loner, thrust into a situation she was almost totally unprepared for. The knife and fork problem was easily dealt with, but symptomatic. Much more important had been our lack of regular contact with other children, particularly in my case with little girls. I had never had a 'best friend' — never in fact any friend of my own age. I was scared of girls — didn't understand them, didn't know how to talk to them, was baffled by giggling and private jokes. I was terrified of doing the wrong thing, of being made fun of. It was impossible for me to join a group, and since most of these girls had been together for two years they were all in groups, and I must have seemed very strange. Like most shy people, too, I must have seemed 'stand offish'.

In all my two years at that school I never made a friend. The teachers liked me — I was no trouble, did well in all my classes, seemed (I suppose) to have no problems. Some of them mistook my quietness and good behavior for leadership qualities and responsibility. Neither were true. When I was occasionally left in charge of the class as the teacher left the room for a short time the orderliness rapidly disintegrated. How could I control the others when I was terrified of them? And on my own I was no more virtuous than any of them. I have a distinct memory of sneaking another girl's textbook off her shelf when I couldn't find mine, and lying quite happily when accused of doing so.

Just once, in those two years, I was brave. It was in my second year, when we'd lived in Exmouth long enough to get to know a neighbor girl who traveled with me on the bus to school each morning. She had never been part of our 'gang' — all boys apart from me. She was pale and thin, one of those people whose eyebrows and eyelashes were white as her hair. Her mother was a strange woman who kept bees, and was usually only seen with a black net veil on her head, going out to her hives. None of us ever went into her house, on a street where we all knew each other.

I didn't really like Veronica, and though we sat together on the school bus we rarely talked together. One day she threw up on the bus. The poor thing had looked paler than usual that morning, and did it without any warning, leaving a smelly mess in the aisle. There was immediately a chorus of condemnation, and Veronica shrank even further into her seat. I took her to the nurse when we arrived, and she didn't reappear that day.

At recess the girls all gathered round to pick up our snack of bread and 'dripping' — the fat from the roast beef of the day before. They started to talk about Veronica, and her 'disgusting' behavior. "Let's send her to Coventry!" someone suggested. This was the custom of shunning a person who for some reason offended the crowd. Most people shouted "Yes!" There was a silence as they looked at me. "What about you, Susan?" one asked. "No!" I said.

So they sent me to Coventry too. It wasn't bad; I felt virtuous, having done something that wasn't really difficult, and knowing I was right. In any case, I still wasn't truly virtuous, not being truly kind. I didn't make friends with Veronica even though she probably needed a friend as much as I did. Perhaps more, because I had my gang of boys and my interesting family. But the other girls were unfair, and I couldn't stand it.

Most of those two years at school passed in a blur. Home was distinct; nothing at school was so important. There were bad moments — the time I forgot to get off the bus because I was reading (that was when I was taking the public bus because the school had had to give up its own) and ended up in downtown Budleigh instead of at my school stop. I was terrified of getting into trouble, so ran to my grandmother, who walked me to school and pacified my teacher. Then there was the day my mother decided not to braid my long hair, which created a panic at school, where hair had to be tightly controlled or cut 'above the collar' — I was immediately taken to the sick bay, where the nurse braided it, and sent me off looking presentable again.

Nothing awful — just constant discomfort, ameliorated occasionally by episodes like the day when the whole school went off on a picnic in a forest. That was the day that the authorities removed the bomb in the field behind us, and we had to evacuate.

It was a real forest, with huge oak and beech trees, and in its midst a clearing, where rope swings hung from high up branches, and you could swing right up into the leaves. I went highest, and it was fun, for once, to be with the other girls. And the Christmas carol service in the

102

chapel, and art classes — these were new and interesting. It could have been worse.

That school closed when the boarders stopped coming because of the fears of invasion on the South Coast, and I went to a much less rigid place.

Meanwhile, Howard didn't go to school at all. He was nearly seven, and had missed most of a year. He still loved plants and animals — particularly animals — and would pour over books with pictures of birds and butterflies. But he had never developed the love of reading that helped me so much during those years. Both of us were abnormally conscious of the emotions and hidden conflicts of these months with our grandparents, but I could shut them out to some degree and bury myself in a book. Howard depended more than I did on the happiness of those around us, and had the need to help — which was impossible. People would keep telling him "You're the man of the family now" and he took it seriously. He probably missed our house in Purbrook, our cat and our tortoise, and our grandparents there. And he had to put up with me as well — competitive, demanding, always planning something he didn't really want to do.

I don't think I got annoyed with him for not always doing what I wanted, but I certainly wasn't sympathetic.

Richard, on the other hand, seemed to like being organized — 'bossed', my mother would have called it. He enjoyed the games and expeditions I planned, and was now a good companion. So Howard probably felt lonely, with nobody who really understood him. Though I at least shared his worries about our father.

It wasn't until we were settled into our new house that Howard went to school, and then it wasn't a success.

My mother in Spain – maybe 1930.

My Parents before I was born – 1930.

My parents on their wedding day– John Owen Goodenough Hayter
& Emma Eugene Masson - December 4, 1931.

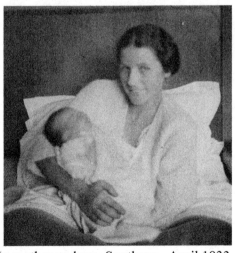

My mother and me, Southsea - April 1933.

Early beach picnic – me and mum.

My father and me – 1935?

My father, me and Howard.

Tea in the garden at Rosyth, Purbrook.

Our home, Rosyth. London Road,
Purbrook, Hampshire – 1935-1941.

A new baby brother, Richard.

Mudpies! Why the Russian hat?

Howard and Susan – probably 1938.

Starting the tiger path – must have been prickly!

Family gathering in Exmouth, Devon, with Hayter grandparents, and my cousins from Spain and Scotland. 1938.

Susan, Cousins Prudence and Jean Logie,
Howard, Exmouth, 1938.

On the beach at Sandown, Isle of Wight, 1939.
With Howard and my new friend.

Typical Richard in our father's boots – 1939.

Taken with my father's little Zeiss camera at arm's
length – an early 'Selfie' – Christmas 1939.

Christmas 1939, with our presents.

Our last family portrait. My mother in the green silk
dress from Hong Kong. Rochester, Kent – March 1940.

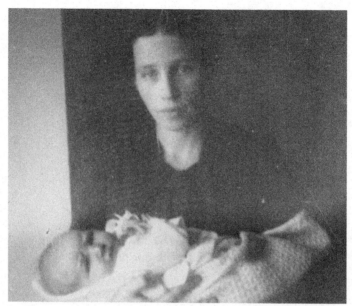

My mother with Sarah, 1941. Perhaps the only photo
my father took of Sarah – just before he left.

The gang by the Hut – Richard, Bobby Pratt,
Hugh Pratt, Howard. Exmouth, 1944.

Susan at Westwood, the Broadway, Littleham Cross,
Exmouth, 1945. In my first 'Shorts'.

Us four, Exmouth, 1943.

The New House

The new house brought us a new life. Our summer and autumn with our grandparents had been full of pleasures. Being with two people who loved us and showed it by learning our likes and dislikes, hugging us, talking to us, even buying us things we really longed for, was warm and comfortable. The other relatives were welcoming and interesting. But opposed to the happiness of all this was the misery of our mother, which was obvious, almost palpable, to at least Howard and me. She was still the most important person in our lives. It wasn't just that she had, in a way, detached herself from us. It was also because she was so uncomfortable in her in-law's home, and so antagonistic to our grandmother, that we felt unable to respond fully to Grandpa and Grandma's affection. Subconsciously we knew this would not please our mother, and we wanted above all things to make her happy. We still had nobody to talk to about our father, because it was obvious that this was a forbidden subject, but far more important was our sorrow that our mother was so different — had become a different person.

Gone was the mother who had charged confidently into cowsheds, requesting a mug of fresh milk from the farmer. Gone was the young woman who'd raced us and always won. When we went for walks that summer she trudged along silently pushing the pram, rarely speaking or pointing anything out. There was one particular walk I remember.. It was a dark, foreboding day, the sky heavy with cloud — a day like many summer days in the damp West Country. There were thunderstorms on the way. We walked up a lane past two thatched cottages, under a tall, echoing railway bridge that our Carter cousins had called 'The Magic Portal', past a farm or two, some gates opening onto fields of cattle, and on to a couple of large ponds, overarched by a red clay cliff on the far side. The water was deep brown, still, and surrounded by rushes and brambles.

Normally we would have played in the water, or explored the whole shoreline. But on that day the place had a haunted feeling — too silent, too dark to be welcoming, especially when combined with our mother's detachment. That day we were glad to leave, and never did go back to play until much, much later. On the way home, however, we brightened up. There was a tiny stream bubbling along beside the road, and since our mother wasn't watching we walked straight into it, not bothering to remove our socks and red Startrite sandals — and she never even noticed. That was the scariest thing of all.

It's strange that I have no memory of leaving our grandparents and their house in Budleigh. Yet I remember vividly so many details about the new house, and our first few days there. I loved that house, though my love for it never prevented me from longing to get away and explore unknown places. But I never felt trapped there, as I had begun to do in Purbrook. That was because suddenly our lives changed.

Changes

We moved into our house in December, and Joyce came with us. Everything was new and different — we too were new and different. Most of all our mother was different. Suddenly she took control of our lives again — she was talking, planning, noticing what we were doing.

The very first day, I remember, we children were sent down to the group of little shops by the railway station to buy a loaf of bread. We felt very grown up and independent. We had never done such a thing before. It was the first sign that things were going to be different from now on. It was a short distance, just down our street, and along another to the right — perhaps a five minute walk in all — and of course there was almost no traffic because private cars were all stored away for 'the duration'. But we were only eight, seven and four. Of course we did fine, and came home throwing the loaf to each other, (no wrapping then) until finally it was dropped on the ground. We scooped it up, of course, something we never told our mother. We didn't think much about germs! There were, after all, no noticeable signs of contamination, though cows passed up and down the street.

As well as being a sign of our independence, this showed that Joyce was not going to be our nursemaid or guardian. She had not been sent along to look after us. From now on, we were often sent on errands, allowed to play in the street, visited friends whenever we wanted to.

The first night in our house felt strange — cold and empty, full of shadows we didn't know. I didn't want to go to bed on my own. "Why are you scared, Susan?" my mother said. "This is our house now." And by the next night it felt like it — it was home.

I had a bedroom to myself — the first time ever — and the boys shared another. Joyce had a little room next to the bathroom. There

118

wasn't much space in it, but it had pretty wallpaper with apple blossoms all over, and probably it was the first room she ever had to herself. My mother had the biggest room, looking out across the front garden and the street. Sarah still slept with her. There was a gas ring on the floor in one corner, where each morning she heated a tiny saucepan full of water to make her early morning tea. Sometimes we all shared it, drinking from the saucer like kittens. And once, later on, Richard knocked over the pan of boiling water and scalded his foot. It was one of the only serious injuries of our childhood.

On the side of the house was a glassed in porch, with a letter box in the door. My mother said that if a German came up to the house (there was still fear of invasion) she would get her carving knife and stab him through it. Although this seemed a bit impractical, given the size and position of the letter box, it was vaguely reassuring. We certainly believed in her willingness to perform such a bloody deed!

Under the stairs was a closet, into which we all crowded when there was an air raid. There were many fewer raids in Devon, but sometimes they were close enough that we could hear explosions. And the bathroom window upstairs looked up to the North, where the ancient cathedral city of Exeter lay. One night, soon after we arrived, we watched Exeter burning, a vast red glow in the sky. Its medieval center, mostly wooden buildings, was entirely destroyed in that raid. These raids have been almost entirely forgotten by the rest of the world.

Although there was a pretty living room, with our familiar cretonne covered chairs and sofa in it, and the carved rosewood tables my father had brought back from China, the most important room in the house was the kitchen. Like most kitchens built at that time — probably about 1900 — it had an open fire, a big scrubbed wood table in its center, and open cabinets for crockery and appliances at the end facing the fireplace. In the center of the cabinets was the gas stove, and to its left was the large, ugly radio.

It was warm in the kitchen, so we spent almost all our time — whatever was left from outside activities — either playing games, drawing or doing homework on the table, or, in my case curled up on the old rocking chair by the fire and reading.

Food preparation wasn't done in there, only the cooking. Peeling potatoes, chopping onions or slicing apples were done in the scullery next door, which also had a large sink, an old copper for boiling laundry, and a larder where all food was kept.

In one way our house was more primitive than the Purbrook house. It still had gas lighting. But we had become used to that in Rochester, so it wasn't much of a shock. And in fact it was an advantage now, because in an air raid the electricity would often go off for quite a long time. The gas would stay on all the time, so when the 'all clear' sounded we could light ourselves back to bed. There were, of course, problems with being without electricity. My mother had to find a gas iron for our clothes, all of which needed ironing. This wasn't easy, but she found an old one for sale. And the huge ancient radio ran on an 'accumulator' which had to be recharged regularly. This was a nuisance, because it took time, and the radio was on almost all the time.

It's hard to exaggerate how important the radio was during the war. Of course there was the BBC News, announced by the tune "Liilibulero" then by names that became as familiar to us as our own — Richard Dimbleby, Alvar Liddell, Stuart Hibbert. Usually my mother and Joyce listened to the 9 o'clock news, and I could hear it faintly from my bedroom, immediately above the kitchen. It was a comforting, regular sound. During the day there were cheerful programs aimed at war workers, like Workers' Playtime, and Tommy Handley's 'ITMA' ("It's That Man Again") Music lightened the atmosphere, often the ribald songs which we didn't really understand, but laughed at all the same — Gracie Fields and "The Biggest Aspidistra", and George Formby, with the slightly smutty song "When I'm washing Winders—".

And then there were the lovely, nostalgic songs like "The White Cliffs of Dover" and "A Nightingale Sang in Berkeley Square", and best of all, a song that always brought tears to my eyes and still does — Noel Coward singing 'London Pride". On Sunday evenings we all listened to my mother's favorite program "Palm Court" with all the old romantic music she loved.

Best of all, " Children's Hour" brought us classic children's books read aloud.

All of these can bring back the feeling of the time, and the cozy kitchen with all of us in it.

We still did not have a refrigerator — shopping for perishables had to be done almost every day, and the milkman left bottles on our doorstep every morning, touring the neighborhood with his horse and cart. But almost everything we needed was just around the corner, so daily expeditions to the baker, the butcher, the greengrocer were very easy.

I am quite sure that even though we had just moved in, our Christmas that year was the same as ever — not, perhaps, as lavish as it sometimes had been, but with all the important ingredients — the paper chains, the holly, the tree, the stockings on our beds and the presents under the tree. Mistletoe would hang from the landing above the hall. There would have been roast chicken and roast potatoes and vegetables and a flaming Christmas pudding and nuts and ginger wine. I know there must have been, or I would have remembered. My mother would have 'scrounged' them somewhere, but in any case special rations were allowed for Christmas. The government was good at maintaining civilian morale.

But never, never, could we have second helpings. There wasn't enough, not even at Christmas. If there was some chicken left it would be kept for the next day, to be used for lunch. We were certainly not starving, but we were always hungry.

That Christmas merged into others in my mind — the main difference being that our presents became increasingly utilitarian or hand made. Not that we cared. Presents were exciting anyway. Eight months after our father's disappearance our lives were returning — not to normal, but in some ways changing for the better.

Perhaps it was partly because my mother had felt out of control while with our grandparents that she had been so unhappy there. She was used to being master of her own household, and didn't have enough to do. And everything my grandmother did was done so differently, and often worse. The house was certainly not up to my mother's standards of cleanliness, for example. Nobody polished the doorknobs there. The sinks were not perfectly white and shining; it was not expected that we should have clean clothes every day. But perhaps none of it really made any difference. She would have been miserable wherever she was.

Now, with a household to manage, four children and an insecure teenager to look after, she started to function again. In our new house we went back to our walks, finding every lane and footpath in the area, pulling and pushing Sarah in the pram through puddles and rutted red clay. My mother began to talk to us again. And one special day she started to run. We were walking towards Littleham Village, a hamlet with an ancient and beautiful church, a parsonage, a smithy, a dairy that still sold ice cream, and a few thatched cottages. The road sloped downhill, then briefly up again.

As the pram began to roll downhill my mother began to run with it. Soon she was chasing along, hair escaping slides and clips, high heels hardly touching the ground. Her voice floated back to us. "Let's race!" we heard. With joy, we followed, pounding along in our Wellington boots, never able to catch up with her, until she stopped, panting, smiling and laughing with baby Sarah, who thought all this a great joke. And we laughed too, happy again — and feeling perhaps, as I did, "It's going to be all right, it's going to be all right.."

Adaptation

Of course it was not quite all right — never would be. Certainly we were all happier because our mother seemed more as she had been before. But for me there was the sadness of knowing that our grandparents missed us, and longed to see more of us. Since I still went to Copplestone House School, next door to them, I was allowed to have tea with them every Friday. Beyond that we seldom saw them, and I don't believe they ever came to see us in Exmouth. I am quite sure that is because they were never invited. But every Friday my grandmother would ask me when we would all be coming over, and I could see the disappointment on her face when I couldn't tell her. Occasionally I would dare to mention these requests to our mother, but she brushed them off with some vague reply.

Those Friday teas were important to me. They continued for the next eighteen months, until the school closed for lack of boarding pupils. Parents were still too scared to send their daughters to the South Coast, where German planes could zoom in from the sea, drop a few bombs, and escape unharmed. But during that time I could run next door to my grandparents after school, and be 'spoilt' for an hour or two every week. We had special treats like stewed gooseberries and custard, which I loved, potato cakes, my favorite 'Scotch Eggs' — hardboiled eggs encased in sausage meat and deep fried. They had time to listen when I talked about school, or my plans for adventures with my 'gang'. And when I left to walk the half mile or so to the bus stop Grandma would often slip a pound note into my hand, a contribution towards my savings for a bike.

Sometimes we did go over to Furzebank, chiefly those occasions when aunts, uncles and cousins were visiting. But during most of the war that didn't happen. Aunt Marjorie and her family were in Scotland, too far away to travel when transportation was so difficult. Janet and hers were in Madrid, having returned there after the Civil War, and just in time to take refuge from wartime England. Jimmy was in the Tank Corps, entertaining the troops. And Francis was in the Air Force, somewhere in the Middle East.

During that time Francis met a young girl in Cyprus whose parents had taken her to live there after she had developed polio. They hoped that the warm climate would help her recover full use of her legs — and in fact she ended up with only mild disability. When Cyprus was in danger of invasion the family moved to South Africa. Francis had fallen in love with her on their brief meetings, and when he suddenly appeared in South Africa on leave they got married. It was 1941; she was only 19. Francis wanted to take her back to England, and that summer they got passage on a troopship, and made the long, roundabout route north, zig zagging all the way to avoid U-Boats. It was their honeymoon, Zoe told me. But as well as the discomforts of the voyage Francis had just heard of our father's death. He had adored and admired our father, his big brother, and loved my mother and all of us. He was apparently devastated, and talked about us all the time. It didn't make for a happy journey, and landing in wartime England can't have been any better. Zoe hadn't lived there since she was a small child. She was only 10 years older than I was.

Soon after we had moved to Exmouth Zoe arrived at Furzebank to meet her in laws. Francis was off in the Air Force again. And we went over to see her– several times, as I remember. She was young, sweet and pretty. We loved her from the start, and she loved us. Perhaps we were a relief from her grief stricken in laws, so much older than herself. And my mother felt protective towards her, and made special efforts to make her feel at home. Zoe gave me a manicure, something that hadn't been (and isn't!) a high priority in my life. I can't say I enjoyed having my cuticles pushed back, but the attention was wonderful. She went away soon, and we didn't see her for ages, but she was a shining spot in that period.

There was one more relative whom we met once at Furzebank, and never again. But we remember her with affection. She was Uncle Jimmy's beautiful wife Marjorie. She visited Furzebank while we were there, spending hours with us, taking part in our games, always willing to play the prostrate enemy or the wicked witch. She was an actress on the London stage, and a perfect playmate. I overheard a conversation on the phone between her and Uncle Jimmy. It was sprinkled with the usual 'darlings' and 'sweethearts' but it was obviously not a happy chat. And I wondered how it was possible to call someone 'darling' in such an unfriendly way. Soon after that they divorced. The family story was that he wanted children — she did not — but I expect there was more than that. Anyway, he went on to marry a young woman who already had one child, and produced seven more for him — so maybe it was partly true. We always wanted to meet her again.

One of the biggest changes in our lives was the presence of Joyce. She wasn't with us to be our nursemaid or nanny. She was there chiefly to help my mother with the things Mum did not like to do — cooking, some housework, laundry, sewing (our clothes were always needing mending). But they worked together on all this. My mother was a hard worker — so was Joyce. Some things ended up being almost exclusively Joyce's, like cooking, baking and sewing. The endless washing, polishing, dusting were always shared. And Joyce did almost everything with us, meals, outings of all sorts, the rare movies we went to — she was our older sister. The only things she didn't share with us were visits to friends and family, at least unless she knew them well. She was still too shy, and felt out of place. And of course my mother probably needed some privacy too.

But Mum had always had strong feelings for 'lame ducks', and whatever had happened to Joyce to make her so quiet and shy must have qualified her for that sympathy and compassion. I don't remember my mother ever got annoyed with Joyce, as she did with us. Joyce never was the focus of 'the look', as Richard called it, when my mother would fix us in an icy gaze that scared us more than any reprimand. And it wasn't that Mum showed her any special attention or affection that might have made us feel left out. She simply accepted her, and we did too. She was part of our family — not quite an older sister, but close. And this happened so fast — she was simply part of our new existence from the start.

Something that seems strange in retrospect was that Joyce didn't have any accent that distinguished her from us. She came from a family which probably would have been described as 'working class'. At that time it really was true, as Henry Higgins says in "My Fair Lady", that "An Englishman's way of speaking absolutely classifies him." It was easy to tell where people came from, and what class they were. But Joyce's parents were fine, hard working people who had jobs that were merging towards middle class — her mother was housekeeper for the Nurses' home in the big house, and her father was the head gardener. One of Joyce's sisters had a good civil service job — the other went to university. So they were 'upwardly mobile' as one might say today.

We never noticed anything different about Joyce's speech, and if it had been different we would have remarked on it, simply out of curiosity. Despite that, we did notice that when our part time gardener, old Gatter, who himself spoke almost incomprehensible Devon dialect, invited Joyce to tea, he never invited us. So other people recognized that she was not quite part of the family.

For the first time, we were free to make our own friends. In my case, perhaps I should say playmates rather than friends, because I never had a real girl friend, someone I could talk to about anything. But even self chosen playmates were a big advance for us. Mine were nearly all male, but that had its advantages later on, because I was always comfortable with men.

Our street, and those around it, were full of children. Next door, just the other side of my mother's bedroom wall, in fact, were two boys. One, the older one, Hugh, was the same age as me. The younger one, Bobby, was about Richard's age. Their father was rarely home either, but at least he was alive. He was off in a desk job in the Air Force, and probably could have come home more. When we did catch sight of him he seemed serious and boring. But his wife, Mary Pratt, was the opposite. She was younger than our mother, with dark curly hair and a smiling face, showing crooked teeth which didn't take away from her charm. Her son Hugh was quiet, rather like his father, but he was friendly too, and happy to join us in all our games. Bobby was a sweet, plump little boy, with big dark eyes. These three became our best friends on the street.

Mary Pratt was completely different from my mother. She had grown up in Exmouth, and was a real local girl, who had never been anywhere much, didn't read extensively, wasn't much interested in the outside world. But for some reason these two women became fast friends. Both were lonely, both needed a friend. But they both had an irreverent view of life, and a rather ribald sense of humor. And perhaps their differences made them more interesting to each other. Because they were both fundamentally bright women, stuck with children and all the multifarious duties and challenges of running a house and family in a war that was affecting everyday life more and more. Neither of them were groaners or the opposite, the vocally 'chin up', patriotic types who most irritated my mother. They simply got on with their lives as they had turned out to be, grabbing every opportunity for fun and adventure, laughing a lot at the ridiculous nature of some of the wartime restrictions.

Mary, whom of course we called Mrs. Pratt, was much less formal and more approachable for us children than my mother was for other children. We wandered in and out of their house quite freely. It was not as perfectly clean and tidy as ours was — we didn't have to worry about stepping on newly polished floors or dropping crumbs on the carpet. When I ran out of reading matter I would wander over to the Pratts and borrow one of Hugh's books. I often liked boys' books better than girls' — there was more action, more excitement. Once when the Pratts were out I climbed in at an open window and picked out a book. Even Mary Pratt was a little put out by that, though more amused than angry. Nobody would have done that with our house. Even though all our friends loved our mother they only entered our house upon invitation. There was always that 'look'.

We soon knew everyone on the street. There was Veronica Chevalier, the pale, quiet girl with the bee keeping mother. They lived across the street. Next door to us, on the other side from the Pratts, were a kind, elderly couple, the Sampsons, who had been evacuated from Kent when that area was being shelled from France. My mother immediately made friends with them, and they would be invited in for tea, or have chats together over the low bank that divided our gardens. Sarah became attached to their black Scottie dog Annie. We gave her a toy black dog that she called Annie too, and dragged around with her on a string as soon as she started to walk. This couple were later replaced by the Thompsons, who had been 'bombed out' of their house in another part of Exmouth. Since they had two children their needs took precedence over the Sampsons, and the Sampsons had to move elsewhere. We didn't think much of that change. Their son,

Michael, was a boring red headed child, not adventurous at all, and a poor exchange for Annie.

Further down were the Fergusons, a Dutch couple, refugees who had managed to get out before the Nazis invaded. Perhaps one of them was Jewish. We had no idea. What we did know was that father and son Eric, were brilliant. Mr. Ferguson had been a professor in the Netherlands, and Eric was obviously going to follow in his footsteps. He was about twelve when we arrived, and already know everything about everything, or so it seemed to us. He would interrupt an evening conversation with an excited "You see that star up there?" and point at some faint dot whose name he already knew. He was far beyond us, and though we made fun of him, with his Dutch accent and not quite perfect English, we were slightly afraid of him. He was too different. We never asked him about his country or his experiences — but then we never asked anyone things like that. We were too concerned with each day, and how we would fill it.

There were two older girls across the street, who sometimes rounded up the younger ones and organized some competition. Making miniature gardens, I remember, was one such venture. Mine had a pond made with a piece of broken mirror, and I thought it very pretty, but it didn't win.

Other neighbors were known by name and spoken to on the street, but we didn't know them well. There were other children, many of them, on the main road that crossed ours a few houses up, and we played freely with them too, but they were not part of our regular games. More often they were designated as enemies, with whom to have battles, which often turned out to be not quite non violent!

All of this could not have been more different from our lives in Purbrook, just eight months ago when we moved in. Even though we now had both my mother and Joyce to watch over us, we were not watched at all for most of the day. Meal times were strictly kept, but since we were always hungry that wasn't much of a restriction. Bed times were still long before we wanted them, but we were usually so sleepy after our days outside that we went to sleep easily. And we still went for walks with our mother or Joyce every afternoon, whether we wanted to or not. Our mother was still the boss, someone you never answered back to, or visibly disobeyed.

We angered her easily in those days. But her anger wasn't expressed in shouting at us, or slaps. It wasn't a sudden anger, over in just a few minutes. It was a cold, silent withdrawal from us — no words, just 'the look' — and it could last a long time. Once, while her friend May Wroe was staying with us, we spilt a bottle of ink on the upstairs carpet. We watched in horror as the black pool spread, and in trepidation ran downstairs to tell her the awful news. With lips tight, cold eyes, no words or comments, we could only watch silently as she mopped up the mess. The carpet, of course, was never the same.

But it was, of course, an accident, and I could see, from the sympathy in May's eyes, that she saw that, and was sorry for us. And that time my mother recovered fast.

I think, perhaps, the perfection of her house, her polished floors, her immaculately made up beds (we learned to do that fast!), her clean, shining children, gave her a feeling of comfort and security. There were never clothes strewn around our bedrooms, or toys scattered in the dining room. A visitor could arrive any time and find a well ordered household.

But every now and then she returned to her former self, the mother who had sung us music hall songs, recited nonsense rhymes, made us laugh with her teasing and jokes. One day a dress came back from the cleaners, a green silk dress that she had loved. My father had brought it back from China. It was a great luxury; silk was expensive. Now, when she tried it on it had shrunk so far it reached mid thigh and clung to her tightly all over. The first we knew of this was the sight of her shimmying round the front lawn, showing it to Mary Pratt, laughing uncontrollably as she pranced and kicked her legs in the air. We gazed in puzzlement. Wasn't she sad? She was, of course, but not so much as to lose her sense of humor.

That was the dress she was wearing in the formal photograph taken just before we left Rochester, all of us solemn, grouped around our seated mother, our father standing behind, resplendent in his dress 'blues'. I was sad for her, but she never said anything more about it.

The lives I'd read about in "Bevis" or the Arthur Ransome books seemed much more possible now, and I began to haunt the local bookshop and libraries in search of more books that told of children who lived adventurously. Books like that barely seem to exist now. Adventure seems largely to take place in a fantasy world — "Harry Potter" or "Star Wars" or "The Hunger Games" — and perhaps this is because a world in which children are actually allowed to explore on their own without adults doesn't exist any more either. There were many books in my childhood that told of children who went camping alone, sailed boats on their own, searched for the sources of rivers, climbed mountains. And those were the things I wanted to do. We were now in an area where I could at least make a start on doing them, and our family dynamics had changed so much that there wasn't much hindrance.

Those Four Years

How strange it is that less than a year after the letter about our father had arrived we should be adapting cheerfully to a new existence! With some surprise, I have to admit that the next four years were some of the happiest of my life. I wonder if I should confess that! It sounds as if the rest of it was without color, or love, or adventure, or accomplishment. But what does make up happiness? At different stages of ones life there are different needs, different pleasures, different aims and achievements. Of course there were many periods of my life when in many respects I was happier, when I felt I was achieving more, loved more and was surrounded by more love, had less worry and more contentment.

I was still continually worried during this time. There was the mystery of my father's disappearance from our lives, and the eternal concern about our mother — our need to keep her happy. There was the ever present fear of more bombing, and the fear for our mother's safety. If she was ever a moment late from shopping or any other outing I would imagine all the things that could have happened to her — traffic accidents, unexploded bombs, sneak air attacks. If she was ever ill I couldn't relax until she was better.

I did not feel specially loved at this time. I doubt if Howard did either. It was very easy to annoy my mother, and I did it frequently. I was beginning to develop my own ideas, and was not slow to express them. I wandered further, stayed out longer, broke even the flexible boundaries she allowed. I planned activities that didn't fit in with her own.

Sometimes those activities were intended for her pleasure. For her birthday the first year in Exmouth we wanted to do for her the things that she had always done for us. We were never allowed to help with the cooking, so couldn't make her a cake, and we had no money to buy one. Presents were easy — we could make bouquets of wildflowers, or drawings, or I could sew a handkerchief. But a party seemed a possibility. It was my idea, of course, and I may have sensed that it might go wrong, because I never even told Joyce about it — I never liked my plans to be deterred. So I wrote notes to the parents of each of our new friends, inviting them to tea on my mother's birthday. These we delivered to their houses.

Of course, I did not think of the logistics of this project. I didn't even know how to make tea, let alone where the cakes, sandwiches and other required delicacies were coming from.

We heard nothing from the parents. But close to the day my mother called me in, grim faced. "What's all this about a party, Susan? I just heard that Mrs. Howard is coming to tea on my birthday. Did you know about this?"

Well, of course I did, and my face probably showed it. She said not a word, but I got 'the look' and a few minutes later I heard her on the phone, calling the parents to explain that there had been a mistake.

I can understand her annoyance. She hardly knew any of these parents. They were not her friends. We had wanted to please her, and I'm still surprised that she didn't seem to appreciate this, even later on. But all of us were already casualties of the war.

Despite all this, I still say those four years were happy. And why? Because, I think, I was more free to do all those things I really loved and enjoyed than at most times of my life. I had compensations.

School, though I disliked most of the things that other girls seemed to enjoy, was completely undemanding and sometimes, as in English, music and art, actually pleasurable. And my mother was always pleased when my report card came back, full of high marks and complimentary remarks about my prowess. So, on balance, it wasn't entirely a negative experience. But in itself, it meant very little to me.

What I really loved was drawing and painting, and at home nobody stopped me from spreading my materials out on any vacant space — preferably the kitchen table — and painting as long as I felt inclined. I painted in watercolors, as taught by Miss Cuddeford, longing to somehow transmit the pleasure I felt in the beautiful countryside around us to paper and paint. I painted all my own greeting cards, and sent them to aunts, uncles and friends. I painted sailing boats, longing to have one of my own, or even just to go sailing, as the Arthur Ransome children did. And my painting was one thing I did that my mother approved of — she admired my efforts, and even arranged for me to have lessons with Mr. Lambert, an old artist who lived up the road.

He taught me almost as much as Miss Cuddeford had. He was a landscape painter himself, but he taught me to look at things in a different way, so that anything could be an interesting subject, if seen in the right way. We started by drawing a slipper, definitely not an attractive object. It was obviously old and well worn, faded brown and creased. I was quite literally shocked that he would want me to draw something so ugly, but I soon became fascinated by those creases, shading them to look as realistic as possible, and ended up discovering that I really liked my drawing, if not the slipper. He showed me the effect of painting in the darks first when working on a landscape, and how to bring light into it by leaving white spaces. He encouraged me to try new ways of doing things.

We even went out in the fields near our house later on, and sketched from life. I still have one of those sketches — across a field to some farm buildings, corn 'stooks' in the foreground. It was a historic painting in a way. One no longer sees stooks — little pyramids of corn stalks in rows across a harvested field. And 'corn' in England meant wheat. Stooks disappeared soon after the war, when combine harvesters took over.

One of my Hayter great aunts, my grandfather's sister Emmie, was an accomplished artist, as was my great grandmother Hayter, who died soon after I was born. Aunt Emmie too was always interested in my painting, and often sent me books on art to study. These were much more interesting than anything I read at school. I learned from her how to draw realistic sailboats, not just those with triangular sails. "Look!" she said. "Don't just copy all the sailboats you've seen in pictures! See what happens when they turn — watch how they look when they're coming towards you."

Mr. Lambert and Aunt Emmie made me watch and analyze, and that was more important than the actual drawing and painting. I did become very good at both, and this was recognized at school and at home. But I realized much later that my aim of becoming a professional artist was not realistic — I wasn't good enough to satisfy myself. I don't know how one recognizes that — it's nothing to do with what anyone else says. I just knew, when I looked at some of my classmate's paintings at boarding school, that there was something about them that I could never attain. All the same, painting remained a major pleasure.

Above everything, our local countryside was a comfort and consolation for most other sadness. I can still go back to it and feel, somehow, that I could wrap myself in it. It envelops me, is so pleasing to my eyes, nose, ears, that I feel warm and secure.

It was particularly lovely during the war. There was almost no traffic, so even if one lived just off a main road, as we did, there was no constant noise — just the swish of an occasional car, or the old Harts bus grinding to a halt, and starting up again with a roar. Sometimes a truckload of Marines would roll down our street on their way to the firing range on the cliffs. They would always be singing — "Roll out the Barrel", or "It's a Long Way to Tipperary" — smiling and waving to us they passed.

Just the other side of the houses opposite us were open fields — green meadows divided by banks and hedgerows. We and the two Pratt boys spent hours there. There was a pond in the corner of the closest field, which would be full of frog spawn, then tadpoles, when spring came. And a small barn, never apparently used, stood in a further field. It was the haunt of spies, we were quite convinced. Spy hunting was one of our favorite occupations. But though we lay on our stomachs behind the nearest bank and watched for ages we never saw one.

These fields, the small woods that punctuated them, the streams that meandered through them, were all ours. Nobody would have stopped us playing in them — evidence of harm was needed for anyone to be prosecuted for trespassing, and we were well trained in country ways. We would never have left a gate open, or dropped rubbish. Our parents and grandparents had seen to that. We knew not to go into fields where there was a lone bull, and not to walk over new crops.

In the mornings, on any day when we didn't have school, we would be out of the house immediately after breakfast, and if we didn't have anything planned in our own garden we'd be out in these fields. They, and the quiet streets around us, were our first playgrounds.

But at first, of course, to go further we needed adult companionship. And with Joyce we had it. She wasn't really adult, but she seemed so to us. Joyce was one of the best things that ever happened to us. I don't think any of us realized until long, long afterwards how lucky we were.

Joyce never seemed to get annoyed with us. She wasn't indulgent — she would tell us when we were doing something my mother wouldn't like — but she never shouted at us or really got upset with us. Not that my mother ever yelled at us either — the 'look' was quite enough! But she never used that look on Joyce, and I can't remember any disagreements between them. It's a strange thing but I can't recall how Joyce addressed my mother. I think it must have been "Mrs. Hayter" since it certainly wasn't "Gene". Each treated the other with respect. They were partners in a way — unequal, but working well together.

Joyce must have sometimes been lonely and homesick. After about a year her sister Mary came to visit. We waited for her on the tiny station in Littleham. Joyce was obviously excited, peering down the line to see if the train was coming, walking up and down anxiously. The train puffed in — passengers stepped out and left the station, the guard's whistle blew — and the train pulled out. Mary was nowhere to be seen. Joyce's face crumpled — she looked as if she was about to cry. My mother put an arm around her. It's all right" she said. "Don't worry, Joyce. She'll just have missed her connection." We went home, and came down again for the next one, and sure enough Mary was on it, also worried about keeping us all waiting.

Joyce adopted us as quickly as we adopted her. It seems as if there was complete acceptance on all sides. She treated us as if she had always known us; we felt the same way about her. She was simply there — calm, quiet, always busy with household tasks or gardening, but also ready to listen when we wanted to talk, or tell us the names of flowers or birds. She was a country girl, who had grown up walking miles across the fields to visit aunts, uncles and cousins. She knew when it was likely to rain, and when it was time to go and look for primroses. There was always some part of the day when she could come out with us, and she wanted to explore the countryside around us as much as we did. So often it was she who took us on our afternoon walks, or sometimes even took me on my own.

And that was how we discovered the beach that became our favorite for several years. And I can't over emphasize the importance of beaches in our lives.

Joyce and I set out one day to find Sandy Bay, a cove in the coast not too far from our house. We'd heard a lot about it. Before the war it had been a favorite place for swimming and picnics. The farmer who owned the fields above it rented out small sections for holiday cabins and camping, but since the war started nobody seemed to go there, and we wondered if we'd be able to get down to it.

The way there led through Littleham Village, a hamlet with a few thatched cottages, a lovely medieval church, a smithy and a terrace of 'council houses' — small dwellings owned by the local council and rented out to low income people. Beyond the village we walked up a narrow, unpaved lane, with high banks on each side. It rose steeply, until at the top we came to the farmyard, with its farm house, barn and cowsheds. Through a gate on the right, into a field sloping downhill, with a muddy track running through it, down to the top of the cliffs and the sea beyond. We could hear the waves by now, and smell the salty air. There were little wooden 'Chalets' dotted around on the grass, but no people at all. Perhaps we wouldn't be able to get to the beach?.

But we were lucky. Above the beach, on the short velvety grass with clumps of sea pinks in it, we discovered that there was a cleft in the red clay cliff that looked manageable. It was obvious we weren't meant to go down — there was barbed wire everywhere and the old steps further along had been destroyed — but that cleft was too tempting. We clambered down it, arriving muddy and a bit scratched on a wide, perfect sandy beach, high headlands and rocks at each end — and nobody there! The waves rolled in peacefully, a few seagulls squawked overhead. It was heaven.

In the summer of 1942 we went to that beach almost every day. Joyce or my mother pushed the big pram with Sarah and all our equipment in it. When we arrived at the top of the cleft we had to unload it all. First came Sarah, in her little sunbonnet. She had to be carried from one to the other down the slippery cliff, to be placed on a blanket on the sand. Then it was the food basket, and finally our swim suits, towels, sweaters and the picnic lunch.

Sometimes we were the only people there. Occasionally it was covered in huge piles of slimy seaweed, which we had to wade through to get to the water. Sometimes it was gray and cold. We didn't mind. There were tide pools in the rocks, filled with shrimp and tiny fish and sea anemones. We took fishing nets, and caught them, but threw them back once we'd shown them to Mum and Joyce. We didn't want to kill them.

None of us could swim, not even our mother. But she liked to wade in the sea, and jump up and down in the waves. And on that flat beach we learned to understand the way water could hold us up. We had rubber rings to wear if we went out too far, and gradually I began to let the air out of mine, until one day there was almost none in it. So just for comfort I tied cords of seaweed round my waist instead — a psychological support. Then I discovered I really could swim, though not in any recognizable style. And however cold I got — and I remember I was sometimes literally blue with cold, my fingers white and numb, I stayed in the waves until I was hauled out by my mother. It was the best thing I'd ever done.

Joyce couldn't swim much either — just a few strokes. But she learnt fast, and both of us tried to copy people we saw who could really swim properly. I never did learn to look elegant or professional, but I could swim for hours, and floated really well.

It amazes me now that we were so free. We didn't even have to wait an hour after lunch to get into the water, as our friends did. Their mothers told them they'd get cramps if they went in too soon — another reason for us to feel superior! Nobody told us that, and we never got cramp. And even after Sarah once fell over in the waves and disappeared under the water — except that her sun bonnet floated on the top so we could rapidly pull her up — we never had anyone looming over us, calling out "Be careful!" We soon learnt to understand the waves, how you shouldn't turn your back on them, how it was easier to get beyond the breakers than to try to swim in front of them. We, after all, didn't want to drown any more than the adults did.

I doubt if my mother really enjoyed the beach as much as we did. It must have been uncomfortable to sit on the sand nearly all day, especially when it was cold and windy. But I don't remember her ever complaining, or making us go home early for her comfort. Perhaps the peaceful place, the cheerful children busy with sand castle building or 'French Cricket' or all our other activities worked as a sort of balm to her.

Sun on our bodies, a warm woolen sweater after a cold swim, the taste of simple food when we were really hungry, the pleasure of discovery — of the natural world, of the skill of swimming — sand between our toes, salt in our hair — all of these became part of our summers those years.

In time we explored other beaches, some of them in town, more of them quiet coves, and much later we abandoned Sandy Bay when it became crowded.

The Waning Days

Even at Sandy Bay there were more reminders of war than the barbed wire and the ruined steps. There was a firing range up on the eastern cliffs, and usually there was rifle fire clattering against the sound of the waves. Sometimes our mother told us we would have to go for country picnics instead, because German planes had taken to swooping in on beaches and shooting anyone there. Often we heard explosions out at sea, and wondered if battles were taking place and ships were sinking. And in May 1944 we were once again kept away from our beaches. Listening to adult conversations, I heard that bodies were washing up all along the South Devon coast. The cause was hushed up until many years later. The dead were young American soldiers training for the Normandy landings, who had been involved in an exercise at Slapton Sands, about forty miles west of us. German E-Boats had dashed in and attacked, leading to the deaths of over 900 American soldiers. There were so many secrets the adults whispered to each other — we had to use our imaginations to fill in the gaps in our knowledge. This was one time when the reality was worse than what we imagined.

But beyond our days on the beach was the fun of having other children to play with, at any time, and as soon as we went out the door. There were no more formal tea parties with nannies — there were no nannies. They were all off doing war work somewhere — being 'land girls' on farms, or building airplanes or making bombs or even joining the armed forces as WAAFs (Women's Auxiliary Airforce), WRENS (Women's Royal Naval Service) or ATS (Auxiliary Territorial Service). I don't know how Joyce managed to avoid being conscripted for National Service, which started for single women in 1941. But she wasn't, and the relief, unperceived at the time, of not being totally dependent on our mother was tremendous. She also must have had the relief of not being with us all the time — though Sarah was always with her. She could come to the beach, join us in blackberry picking along the lanes, allow us to have friends over for tea, but there was someone to take over occasionally.

Tea with friends was quite different now. Unless we were visiting friends of my mother's — and she soon found that there were several familiar Marine families around — we went on our own, to children we actually enjoyed being with. I'd met a girl called Betty Howard somehow. She was about as close to being a girl friend as I had in those years and I went over to her house regularly. She had a younger sister called Rosalie, a timid child whom we ignored as much as possible. Once, I arrived there to play, only to find that Betty had been banished to her bedroom for some crime and I was made to spend a boring afternoon with Rosalie. But most of the time we had fun, though usually indoors. Betty was an indoor child, and liked playing with paper dolls or dressing up more than climbing trees. We invented home made lotions for our dolls, and discovered we both liked the taste of soap. We became princesses and witches. It was a nice change, though I wouldn't have admitted it to myself. Her mother was a large, imposing woman, who actually had a husband who came home in the evenings. He was a Naval officer, but had a desk job, to my mother's scorn, and he was always referred to by Mrs. Howard as 'Daddy Dear'. So we did too, though rather derisively. On Betty's birthdays he'd show home movies, the best part being when he reversed the motion and people started running backwards uphill.

Betty rarely came over to our house. I think she found my games too scary. But later on, when we were approaching adolescence, I was able to ask her a few questions about my changing body, and she answered quite calmly, informing me that her mother had actually talked to her about such things. It was hard to imagine the formidable Mrs. Howard talking about a subject that seemed to alarm my mother so much. I viewed her with increased respect.

So many children then were described as 'delicate'. Heaven knows what that actually meant — they seemed healthy enough to us. But since we almost never got sick we looked down on those children. It wasn't their fault, of course, that they weren't allowed to play our rough games. But it meant that we didn't look forward to being with them, which happened when our mother made friends with a Marine wife whose children fit into that category. Their names were Margaret Ann and Neville, and tea parties there were dreary. There was a small, tidy garden, and nothing much to do. Margaret Ann was my age, with pretty, curly hair, and Neville was Howard's. They never came to the beach with us, and rarely to our house. I think my mother finally stopped taking us to tea there and left us with Joyce. She actually didn't have much in common with Dorothy Pugh, their mother. But she needed the Marine background — someone to chat with about remembered places and good times. These Marine wives weren't always virtuous like my mother. Dorothy later took up with her husband's nephew, another Marine not much younger than she was, and ended up divorced and remarried to him.

Tea in those days was an important meal. For us it took the place of dinner. It was not, however, 'high tea' — a mistake often made by Americans! High tea was something eaten at about five or six, after the working man came home. It was a solider meal than 'afternoon tea', which was something taken by the 'upper classes' or those who aspired to such. This was usually at about four o'clock, so obviously one had to have leisure to enjoy it. We would have sandwiches, scones, biscuits (cookies), cake, and sometimes hot buttered toast — only it was margarine — with jam or honey. And always tea, served in a teapot and poured into cups, never mugs. That would keep us going until a snack before bedtime — a warm drink, cocoa or 'ovaltine', perhaps a boiled egg or toast and marmite. And never, ever, any snacks between meals — except, during the season, apples — and even then we had to ask before we ate one.

No wonder food tasted good!

It was a convenient social meal for women at home, especially during the war. Bread wasn't rationed, margarine took the place of butter, tea (also rationed) could be weak. And in our home it was always quite formal, with a tea trolley spread with a pretty cloth, real china, and little sandwiches with thinly cut bread cut into triangles. It was our favorite meal. And it was easy to produce, and provide for.

We never had 'Dinner'. Lunch was our main meal. Our mother and Joyce would have soup or bread and cheese, tomatoes and celery for supper after we went to bed. And that's what we did too even after the war.

Nearly all food tasted good to us in those days. Seasonal fruits were looked forward to — strawberries, raspberries, gooseberries, only available for short periods. Special treats for us children were fizzy drinks of any sort, only allowed on very rare occasions, and of course, candy. Since candy was so important in England there was a weekly ration, which we picked up at one of the small shops in Littleham. It didn't last long, but was one of the pleasures of life. Later in the war, chocolate became unobtainable, and we discovered that there was a chocolate laxative that tasted fine. But its unfortunate effects made us give it up.

Various recipes went the rounds — ways to make use of unusual ingredients to make up for unobtainable items. Real orange marmalade, which most people eat for breakfast in England, virtually disappeared, because you couldn't get oranges. So Joyce and my mother made a jam out of carrots and orange essence. We didn't like it much, but there was another, made from marrows, a sort of watery squash, and ginger. This was quite good. And so was one made from rhubarb, which grew in everyone's gardens. We all went out picking wild blackberries in the hedgerows. Jams, of course, needed sugar, and extra sugar was allowed during jam making season.

When we went to birthday parties the food was always about the same, because everyone had the same problems. Just sometimes there would be a real iced birthday cake, but often a colored sheet of cardboard in the shape of the cake would be placed on top of it, so that it looked as if it was iced. And cakes didn't taste the same, because eggs were rationed, and there were never enough to make proper cakes.

Mostly we didn't notice changes in our diets, but there was one thing that distressed us all. We'd never had much ice cream, just occasional cones from the Walls Ice Cream Vans that would be stationed by the beaches. Since we didn't have a fridge we couldn't keep it at home. But since we moved to Exmouth and started walking to Sandy Bay we had often stopped at the village dairy in Littleham on the way. It was a bare little store, right opposite the blacksmith's, where we often dropped in to watch the smith, in old corduroys, shirtsleeves and a waistcoat, heating the horseshoes until they glowed red, hammering them on the anvil till they sparked and turned white, then sticking them onto the hooves of a patient cart horse. The raw scent of burning hoof drifted across to the dairy. There, one summer day, we stopped in to have our special treat, an ice cream cone apiece.

This time was different. Myrtle Bell, the girl behind the counter, was sad. "I'm sorry, kiddies" she said. "No more ice cream! The government said so."

We were aghast. This was too much. But my mother saved the day by letting us order sodas, any color we wanted. There was no more ice cream until after the war.

We were wartime children, but shielded from its worst aspects. We were lucky, but it never occurred to us to compare ourselves to others. We were too absorbed in our everyday lives.

War Work — and Other Activities

Every now and then my mother would round us up to work in our 'Victory Garden' though with her aversion to appearing patriotic she never called it that. In fact it was more of a necessity than a patriotic exercise. Home grown vegetables were cheaper, and could be plentiful. And we had Joyce, a gardener's daughter who loved growing things, whether flowers or edibles, to direct the jobs and do most of them. My mother didn't like gardening; we did, up to a point. We certainly didn't like it if it interfered with any of our plans (chiefly mine) for the day, or if it took too long and got boring. It was fun to plant carrots or radishes and watch them come up, and in the mild, damp Devon climate everything flourished. And a carrot just pulled out of the ground and washed very briefly tasted so good, so sweet and crunchy.

We children grew the easy vegetables. Joyce was mostly responsible for the fruit trees and bushes — black currants and red currents, gooseberries and raspberries, strawberries, plums, apples and pears. The plums, pears and some apples grew on espaliered trees along the brick wall that divided our garden from the Pratts. Our garden was backed by a bank with trees growing out of its top — probably part of the old field boundary that had existed before the houses were built. But the Pratt's garden was surrounded by these walls, and our wall met up with theirs and the ones running behind all the other houses leading up to the main road, forming an above ground highway.

We walked along these walls, most of the year just for fun, and to practice jumping off them. But during the fruit season all of them had fruit trees like ours, and we happily stole from them. I don't think we were ever discovered. We'd sit on a wall, our legs dangling down on the least populated side, and bite into delicious, juicy pears and apples. We were careful not to throw cores and pits into the owners' gardens.

Later on we demolished part of the wall between our house and the

144

Pratts' and used the bricks to build a hut in the Pratts' garden. Theirs was much wilder than ours — Mrs. Pratt didn't have a Victory garden. The hut was just big enough for us three and the two Pratt boys to fit into. It had a fireplace and a chimney set into the 'thatched' roof. The roof was dead grass arranged on some old planks. We had brick stools to sit on inside. In that hut we made fires and baked potatoes, usually eating them when they were charred but hard and slimy inside. They tasted wonderful. And I used to 'borrow' my mother's little miniature brass dishes from Holland to cook my own concoctions — usually not as good as the potatoes.

Our mothers never interfered with this obviously dangerous activity. But later in the war, when Mr. Pratt came back, he pulled our hut down one day, without even telling us. I cried all day, and never forgave him. The adults took no notice. Crying was allowable, if not approved: we knew we should not cry if hurt, or if scolded — or, of course, when sad about our father. The destruction of our hut was not considered a serious loss.

Joyce grew flowers. They were her real love. She planted the bed under the kitchen window with all the spring flowers — first snowdrops and crocuses, then grape hyacinths, primroses, violets, daffodils of all sorts, following them with the summer blooms — asters and pinks and scabious and poppies and daisies and foxgloves. It was a medley of color as soon as the weather warmed up. There were always flowers to pick in our garden and out in the hedgerows, and the house was never without them, reflected in the shiny surfaces of the furniture that Joyce and my mother polished daily.

Gardening meant weeding — not popular with us — and pruning, done by Joyce. Both of these resulted in bonfires — one of the joys of life. The autumn was full of bonfires, with their marvelous smoky smell and opportunity to bake more potatoes. They also provided the chance to behave like Australian aborigines and have a 'corroboree' — we three and the Pratts dancing round the fire, clad in what we imagined to be aborigine wear. Once Howard decided that the string of flags we'd used for some festive occasion would make an appropriate lower garment. But he forgot that there were gaps between the flags, revealing much of his naked body. He was probably closer to aborigine attire (or lack of it) than all of us — much to my mother's and Joyce's amusement.

145

Our garden was never a private place. We could bring any of the local children into it — though not the village children. There was always that separation, though the village wasn't far away. But even on our own there was lots to do. There was a large tree stump in the front, just by the green gate with the name of our house on it. The stump must have been about six feet high, and was covered with slippery ivy. I longed to go up it, but at first I was too small and there were no good toe holds. Finally — I must have been nine or ten — I managed to scrabble up it. Few achievements have given me as much pleasure!

The flat top of that stump provided us with a fort, an observation point for our 'wars' with the other local gang, and, for me, a marvelous place to read in peace.

Later we watched for the approach of American troops in their giant trucks, so that we could gather in front and catch the longed for candies they flung at us. So much better than any fake 'climbing structure' and only marginally dangerous, for once.

The other gang was led by a much hated boy called Georgie Fardell, who lived up on the main road. We had no reason to hate him, but we needed people to fight, and to fight them we needed to hate them. Not so different from any war. We had learnt well. In autumn we used 'conkers' as weapons — shiny horse chestnuts — and hurled them at Georgie's gang. Sometimes they tried to capture us, and drag us off to their lairs — but they never succeeded. Though once I remember clinging desperately to a protruding tree root sticking out of a bank while two tough boys tried to haul me off, till they saw an adult coming and ran off.

There were two other centers of entertainment in the garden, the swing and the garden shed. The swing wasn't there when we moved in. My mother found a man who put in two stout tree trunks with a bar across the top. Then she and I went down to the harbor, and up some rickety stairs to a sail loft. She told the sail maker just what she wanted, and soon we had a fine swing, with sturdy ropes and a wooden seat. It was tall enough that you could go really high, and ropes flexible enough to be twisted, so that you could twirl around and get dizzy. We used it for innumerable games and competitions, jumping off at the height of the arc, standing up on it, hanging upside down on the ropes.

The shed was the sort of garden shed found in any garden in England

— a shabby wooden building intended for storage of tools, fertilizers, seed and so forth. On one side an overhanging roof made a good play area for rainy days, and later on for housing our rabbits. But at first it was a home for our 'snailery'. There were snails everywhere — not too popular with Joyce, who stamped on them whenever she saw them. Some of them were very pretty, with pink, white or gold shells. These ones were much smaller than the ordinary brown variety, and they were the ones we collected if we could find them.

Richard and I were the ones most interested in the snails. We kept them in cardboard boxes, and tried out all sorts of food on them. They were interesting and fun, but it was hard to feel affection for them, as we did for our new cat, a gray and white tom called Flippy. Some experiments on them ended in cracked shells, which we sometimes tried to mend. At other times we sentenced them to death and cold heartedly trod on them.

It was very different with our rabbits. Many people kept rabbits in those days, usually to add to their meat ration. But our rabbits were not meant to be meat. I'm not quite sure how old we were when we got them, or how we managed to persuade our mother to let us have them. She already had a cat and four children under ten, and she probably foresaw smelly hutches and arguments and scrambling to find food for them. Perhaps she was right. And I think I was aware that in the case of any default in my brothers' performance with cleaning or feeding I would be held responsible, being the eldest. So I made sure these duties were carried out, and I don't remember them ever being a burden.

That was because I loved my rabbit extravagantly. His name was Blackie — unoriginally since he was black. He was a soft, gentle animal with velvety ears that I loved to run between my finger and thumb. I could pick him up and cuddle him close to me, unlike Howard's gray rabbit, Whiskers, who struggled and bit whenever anyone tried to handle him. Mine seemed to like me. He'd stick his head under my chin and make little whiffling noises, which made me love him even more.

Since in our family children were all treated equally, at least as far as possessions and allowance (which in the latter case meant none for any of us) Richard had to have a rabbit too — a little white baby rabbit. So the only one who didn't was Sarah, too young to look after one.

The rabbits lived in hutches made from wooden boxes with chicken wire doors on their fronts. For bedding we picked grass from along the lanes near our house. They were deep, ancient thoroughfares worn down by centuries of wagons and farm carts, their banks covered with ivy and grasses, and pink, yellow, blue and white flowers in spring and summer.

In summer it was easy to find rabbit food. It was everywhere. We took burlap sacks that had held potatoes and filled them with grass and dried leaves and dandelions and groundsel, the last two being our rabbits' favorite food. It was fun to thrust a bunch of groundsel into the hutch and watch an excited rabbit nibbling furiously, his little nose trembling up and down. I could watch Blackie for ages. It was a peaceful thing to do. He was obviously happy in his neat little home.

In winter I covered it with a worn old blanket to keep out the chill, though all the rabbits had plenty of fur. In fact I sometimes thought they were warmer than we were. It was so cold indoors in those days, when coal was rationed and we could only light the fire in the afternoon. I wore mittens all the time, even at school, but I had chilblains on my fingers and toes, swollen, itching and cracking. But it was normal for winter, just something to put up with.

The main problem with winter was that rabbit food disappeared. The dandelions stopped growing. There was no long grass. We took the carrot peelings from the kitchen, and the outer leaves of cabbage and cauliflower, but it wasn't enough. Every so often Blackie or Whiskers would escape from their cages, pushing away the chicken wire or gnawing a hole in the wood. Perhaps they knew that next door Mrs. Barclay, a widow who lived alone, had a kitchen garden filled with carrots and cabbages. We always found the rabbits there, but usually Mrs. Barclay found them first, and there would be an irate phone call demanding that my mother control her children and their rabbits more effectively.

So eventually, with my mother's tacit assent — because she undoubtedly suspected what we were doing — we took to crime. There were some 'Allotments' — community gardens you could rent to grow food — just up the street. We'd get up early on cold dark mornings and climb over the fence into the gardens. We never took whole cabbages — we just took the outer leaves, pale green and stiff with frost. Surely nobody would miss them? My mother never enquired why we were up so early. We were officially cleaning their hutches. And so they survived till the spring came and the weeds grew again.

I went down one morning to see Blackie. His door was a little bit open — perhaps I'd forgotten to latch it. At first I thought he was asleep — he was just lying there, his soft black fur slightly rumpled. I put my hand in the hutch, but before I touched him I saw. He had no head. No ears, no nose — just a stiff cold body.

I ran for my mother, scarcely able to breathe. And this is strange, but I don't know what she did. Perhaps the loss of a rabbit didn't seem too serious to her. But she didn't suggest getting a new rabbit. She knew, at least, that you couldn't replace someone you'd really loved. Whatever she said or did, I cried all that day, and most of the next one. After that, I stopped, but Blackie's death has remained one of my most vivid memories.

Schools and Other Things

When Copplestone House closed I rushed home carrying a beautiful silver Cup, awarded to me in the last Assembly. It rewarded, improbably, my 'Improvement in Games', meaning netball, rounder's (a game somewhat like Baseball), etc. Somehow I knew that this was not the whole story, though I was excited and impressed to have it. My mother hit on what was probably the reason for my honor. She said it was likely they hadn't really known what to give me — there was no official symbol of appreciation for someone who had consistently been top of her class in everything. Games were always much more important, and were the only thing that earned silver cups, so my reward had to be related to sports. It was good to please my mother, but I knew quite well that it didn't mean much, because I hadn't had to work hard, and I certainly hadn't improved in sports. Everything I'd done had been the result of Miss Cuddeford's good teaching. We had to give the cup back after a year was up. It looked a little battered by than, since it had been dropped once or twice, and Miss Brackenbury sent my mother a rather annoyed little note about that.

That September I went to a new school. It was very different, though not much better academically. This one was called Hythe House School, and it had been evacuated from Hythe in Kent because of the bombing there. It was in a house, just an ordinary tall Edwardian on the way to Exmouth, but bigger than most. So there was no gym, no dining hall, no chapel, no playing fields. There were no boarders. We played hockey and tennis at the Tennis Club across the street. The class rooms were regular rooms, and we went home for lunch. There definitely was no butler! It was homier, more relaxed than Copplestone, and the girls seemed nicer, but perhaps I was just getting used to girls.

There were two 'head mistresses' — a pair of elderly spinsters who were quite pleasant and unthreatening. The teachers were mostly mothers with some sort of academic background, and a few profession-als. None of them were inspiring so once again school was not very interesting. I doubt if there was a B.A. among them, but I'm sure Miss Cuddeford hadn't had one either. I knew you didn't have to have offi-cial qualifications to be a good teacher, but maybe it sometimes helped. Anyway, the real teachers were probably off doing war work.

I began to be invited to birthday parties, and actually enjoyed some of them. The other girls were mostly local, which meant that I got to know families who belonged in the area. I didn't disappear into a cor-ner with a book any longer, but actually took part in the games and competitions. Almost everything, even parties, contained elements of competition, but I didn't really mind that. So school was much more bearable, and I wasn't scared of it any more.

Meanwhile poor Howard, and then Richard, had a much worse experience. They hadn't been lucky enough to have Miss Cuddeford, and their first school was a little place called Woodlands, where they didn't seem to learn anything much I knew that, because I loved to play school with them — myself as the teacher, of course, trying to pass on the things I had learned earlier on. I don't think Howard thought much of that! But soon they changed to a real boys' prep school (in England a prep school is a private school for children between the ages of around eight to fourteen). It had sports fields and class rooms, 'day boys' and boarders, much like Copplestone.

But St. Peter's was far tougher, and misbehavior was punished by caning. Unfortunately, failure to perform well in studies was treated the same way, and poor Howard, who knew so much about birds and ani-mals and followed the news so carefully, was caned regularly for doing badly in tests — particularly in mathematics. He could read and write really well, but suffered badly from nerves when faced with exam ques-tions. The thought of a possible caning can't have helped him. I don't know how much he told our mother about this — probably not much. But he told me that he used to believe our father wouldn't have allowed this to happen to him, and I think he was right. I can't blame our mother for not doing anything. Parents didn't get involved in school affairs much in those days. We were turned over to the 'experts' who were responsible for our educations while under their charge.

Richard, on the other hand, seemed quite content there, and was good at sports, which was always helpful in these schools. And even I enjoyed going there occasionally. We used to go to their plays — very exciting with all those 'big' boys (the oldest not more than fourteen), acting in dramas like "Sanders of the River" by Edgar Wallace, set in colonial Nigeria. I would get totally involved in the action. I had never been to a play in a theater, except for traditional English pantomimes, which I hated because they were so unrealistic. And if for any reason it wasn't convenient for me to go home for lunch I went to St. Peter's. They had lunches that I thought were delicious, especially curries with raisins in them.

So even if school took up most of the day, it was the time spent out of it that remains in my mind — the freedom, the cool damp air, the smells of seaweed and crushed grass, the joys of running full speed downhill and wading in the little streams, the crunch as one bit into a sweet, just picked apple — these were some of the pleasures of that time.

We were blessedly free of other organized activities. An exception was 'Brownies' for me. I have a feeling I must actually have asked to join this group, perhaps because someone I liked at school belonged to it. It was not the sort of thing my mother would have encouraged. 'Brownies' in England was the precursor to 'Girl Guides' — the equivalent, if not the same, organization as 'Girl Scouts' in America. Both Brownies and Girl Guides were geared much more to out door adventures than they are in America, much more based on the Boy Scouts, and were also founded by Robert Baden—Powell. Certainly when I was a Brownie we spent a lot of time practicing knot making, marching along on organized hikes (not nearly as much fun as our own journeys of discovery), reciting the Brownie oath.

"I promise to do my best, to do my duty to God and the King, to help other people every day, especially those at home." I always found this rather embarrassing, not being used to mention of God or duty, and being aware of my mother's amusement.

My group's 'Brown Owl' was our doctor's wife, and his daughter Shirley also went to Hythe House. I liked Shirley, and I liked Dr. Murray too. He was a big, bluff man, very outspoken, who, we were informed, once told our grandmother that she could "live on her blubber for a month". This did not go down well, as one could imagine.

Grandma was comfortably plump, but not in any way obese. Mrs. Murray was a large, impressive woman, with a very loud voice. She took pride in adopting any official recommendation on diet or safety, and to my surprise her living room was full of beds. Having been told at the beginning of the war that it was safer to sleep downstairs she had moved the family beds, five in all, down to their main reception room. I knew nobody else who had gone to such lengths.

Our Brownie meetings were held in the dining room of the Murrays' house. A lot of time was spent making sure our ties were knotted correctly, and our badges sewn on straight. We learned the Brownie salute, and sang patriotic songs. I think I actually lasted until it was time to transfer to the Guides, at the age of ten, but by then I had discovered for certain that I preferred putting up our old pup tent in the garden, even if the ropes were not knotted correctly, than making sure that every crease in the canvas was smoothed out and the pegs hammered in at perfect intervals, as required by the Guides. The emphasis on correctness and conformity didn't suit me.

For some reason Mrs. Murray seemed to like me, and I liked Shirley, and that was lucky, as it turned out later. But meanwhile I returned to my usual everyday adventures.

Questions?

It seems very strange to me now that our father had disappeared so completely from our existence. Why didn't Howard, Richard and I talk about him? We had plenty of chances, now that we were so free and so often out of sight of our mother. It was certainly not that we didn't think of him. I think our vivid memories of him are proof of that. Perhaps the very fact that we kept these memories to ourselves and cherished them individually for years without talking about them is the reason they have remained so fresh in our minds.

The sad thing is that since our mother would not talk about him — maybe felt incapable of talking about him — we somehow felt that there was something shameful about doing so. Other children had fathers, and they talked about them. We had also had one, and he had seemed superior to the others. Why couldn't we even mention him? I didn't know why, but I followed my mother's example, and rarely mentioned him even to Howard.

There were some possible explanations for my mother's silence. First of all, the letter she received on that morning before my birthday — a badly typed document with no words of comfort in it — had told her only that he was 'missing, believed dead'. It had expressly recommended that she should not tell anyone the news, in the 'interests of security'. The government was anxious to boost morale in the country, and to keep the news of British losses from the enemy.

But of course she did tell people — her parents, his parents, her friend May Wroe, and others, I'm sure. First, of course, she needed to. Second, she was not one to accede to unreasonable requests.

Quite soon she received letters from two survivors of the Bonaventure, one from the Captain, one from Turner. Both were kind and distressed. Turner had been able to go on board and had dived off before the ship sank. He was naked, and the water was cold. He and some of the remaining crew members kept afloat until rescued by another British ship. He said that he had seen my father go below decks just before it blew up — that there was no chance of his survival. The Captain confirmed that conclusion.

Despite this, there was no confirmation of his death from the Admiralty until the war was over. So perhaps our mother felt there was some hope, and didn't want to tell us until she was sure.

I've asked many relatives if they knew why she did not talk to us, and none of them knew. Several of them had tried to get her to do it. But again another factor may have been that death was still something that was not discussed with children, and as I have said she rarely answered our questions on anything she found awkward and difficult. Her whole family, with the possible exception of Auntie Iris, was like this, and so, I suppose, were many parents then.

But not all. Once, at the birthday party of a girl I barely knew, I saw a photo of a man in Army uniform on her bedside table. "Who's that?" I asked. " My father. He got killed in the war". It was such a relief to hear her say this. We talked together a long time at the end of the party, telling each other about our fathers, talking about the things we'd done with them, feeling an immediate bond. I left feeling actually joyful, a burden lifted.

I have no idea if my brothers ever had that experience. Probably not, since boys, far more than girls, seldom talk about their feelings. And Sarah probably never even heard our father mentioned in her whole childhood, eventually going to May Wroe and asking her to talk about him. Sadly, my resentment of Sarah continued, fed by the fact the she received the tenderness that I felt I lacked, and had once had.

So this created a chasm between us and our mother. And I think that originally she may have needed this — the space to mourn on her own, not to deal with our worries, perhaps even resentful of our constant presence. She was not the sort of mother one could run to with a hurt or a problem. We all learnt to deal with those on our own. And in time she did begin to notice us more, and try to help.

The greatest compensations to us at this time were Joyce, and our extended family. Despite my one meeting with the girl at the birthday party I still never had a friend who was close enough for me to risk talking about something that meant so much. I needed someone who had gone through the same thing to be comfortable with that subject. But what we did have was many people who loved us, were interested in us, and helped us in many ways.

We saw even less of our grandparents and the Budleigh great aunts once I left Copplestone, but all of a sudden we became very close to some other Hayter relatives, also in Budleigh, whom we'd barely known before. These were two women we'd met before, but who had no children, so seemed less interesting to us than the Carters at Pine Hollow or the Peddies with Ian.

Muriel and Joyce Hayter, the widow and daughter of Frank Hayter, who had died at the beginning of the war, were about fifty and twenty two in 1941. Frank was a New Zealander who had come back to the land of his ancestors when Joyce was a baby. Family gossip told us that this was because Muriel couldn't stand life in rugged NZ, without servants or a nanny. She was from the North of England, with a prosperous family. Frank's father was my great grandfather's brother, a naval captain who had gone off the Antipodes and founded a huge sheep station in the South Island. The famous little church of the Good Shepherd at Lake Tekapo memorializes him and other pioneer sheep farmers. He also was instrumental in building the Hermitage Hotel at Mt. Cook. None of this apparently impressed Muriel, though she later made sure she kept track of its financial success.

Muriel was quite tall, redheaded (though by the time we knew her the color probably came out of a bottle). She was loud and strong minded, and a leader of the local volunteer firefighters. A story about her is that one of the male firemen, annoyed with her overbearing ways, aimed a firehose at her backside, leading to an undignified collapse. But somehow she and my mother became fast friends. Why this was I did not know. Perhaps it was because they had both been widowed at about the same time — and both were on the fringes of the main Hayter clan.

Muriel was hard to like. She was very formal, served lunches we did not enjoy on a beautifully set walnut table, and was generally rather frightening. But Joyce was a different matter. She was pretty and young — another but very different Joyce — and loved to be with us and talk to us. She had been to University, and was teaching part time at a local boys' school. I don't know why she wasn't in the armed forces, but Muriel had probably threatened sickness and death if the question came up — as she did every time Joyce brought home a boy friend. Joyce tried to improve my swimming, in the clear cold waters off Budleigh Beach, and lent me her books. I discovered Sir Walter Scott. A small table in their sunny living room contained shelves of books beneath it, and in that I discovered "Kenilworth". The strange death of Amy Robsart fascinated me, and I read the whole thing. It was so much more romantic and exciting than Dickens, whose "Old Curiosity Shop" I'd already finished. I enjoyed both authors then, and never have since!

Sometimes Muriel would invite us all over for a little vacation. We slept upstairs in their elegant bedrooms, and ate all our meals in the fancy dining room with a big polished table. We would go to the beach every day, and come back salty and hungry, and in time we began to desert Sandy Bay and take the bus to Budleigh and its beach, composed of perfect pebbles smoothed by a great river in Jurassic times. There my mother and Muriel would chat, while we and the two Joyces would swim and invent games with the beautiful pebbles.

Joyce too loved Pine Hollow and the Carters, who had 'adopted' her as they did with all young people. But we only saw them now when we 'dropped in' on our way up the cliffs, or went to sing Christmas carols to them each year.

When later on we all had our embarrassing belated baptisms my mother asked Joyce to be my Godmother. She was only 14 years older than me, but she was a marvelous godmother, never bothering about duties like teaching me my catechism but writing to me all her life and sending me lovely, thoughtful presents on every possible occasion. Every present showed that she knew me and my tastes — a true sign of love. And I wrote to her, so she was a constant presence, even when we didn't see each other for thirty four years of my adulthood.

Muriel was a different matter. I think we were all a little scared of her. She too was my godmother, but we never corresponded in the same way. When we visited them in Budleigh she was often in bed, lying there next to a shelf covered in medicine bottles. Listening to my mother's quiet conversations with Joyce Kinge I discovered that some of those bottles did not contain medicine, but alcohol (unless one considers that curative). None of us thought of it as evil — my mother loved her occasional glass of sherry –but it did seem strange that Muriel should keep it at her bedside.

Despite this weakness she was a good business woman, and started a small operation, "The Home Kitchen" in her own lavish kitchen and adjoining rooms. Of course she did none of the cooking herself — a nice older man, a retired chef called Johnnie, did that. And there was a staff of at least three beyond him. Muriel, however, directed the lot, and Joyce also worked there when not teaching. The aim was to produce fully prepared, ready to eat hot meals for old people, infirm people, and those who simply missed their own cooks, now departed to aid with the 'war effort'. Since plenty of affluent elderly people lived in Budleigh this was surprisingly successful, and continued long after the war. Johnnie was a great cook, very innovative in his efforts to make up for the deficiencies in culinary materials caused by the war, and I'm sure many customers ate better than they ever had.

I sometimes went to the kitchen with Joyce, and loved the friendly, busy atmosphere. I got to know all the helpers, and often went out to deliver meals with Johnnie in the van, visiting large, shadowy houses in neglected gardens. And of course, the elegant meals we ate at the shiny dining room table were not prepared by Muriel's hands!

Two more people, rarely seen, but memorable, were our grandfather's three sisters, Aunts Nettie, Emmie and Kitty. They came to visit their brother about once a year, and stayed in a big hotel (always pronounced, French style, without the H.) My mother said this was because old people had been taught to do it this way. Our grandfather did too, but we had never noticed because he — and we— never stayed in hotels. We stayed with relatives or friends if we ever went anywhere. This hotel was the Rougemont Hotel in Exeter. And I remember that because Aunt Nettie's married name was "De Rougemont", and I thought it must have something to do with her.

All three were tall and dignified. At any rate it seemed that way to me, though I realize they were probably not tall but just very upright, in true Victorian fashion. They were less dignified when with my grandfather, whom they teased as if they were all children again. They also teased Aunt Kitty, the youngest, because she phoned her husband, a retired judge called Uncle Robin, every day. She and he adored each other, and died, much later, within a few days of each other.

But Aunt Emmie was the one I knew best. I think my father must have been a favorite of hers. She had lost her own son in World War I, and perhaps some of her love for him had been transferred to my father. For whatever reason, she paid me a lot of attention on her visits. As well as her interest in my painting she sometimes took me out to lunch at one of the leading local hotels. I was not used to being faced with a full set of cutlery, and had no idea what to use or how to order my meal when the waiter came. I simply ordered an omelet, as did my aunt. I had never had an omelet — they are difficult to make when you only have an egg or two to share among six. The embarrassment came when I used my fish fork to eat it with, again following my aunt's lead. "Dear, I see you also use a fish fork to eat an omelet" Aunt Emmie remarked. It was a kind way for her to tell me that this was not normal, I suppose, but I blushed violently, and felt very 'gauche'.

Although my mother thought I got too much attention from our grandparents, she didn't seem to object to the favoritism from my great aunt. In fact she liked them all, and kept in touch with them and their daughters as long as she lived. And perhaps my brothers didn't mind being left out of those formal meals!

As for our Masson grandparents, we wrote to them regularly, and they wrote to us. Letters would come in my Grandpa's perfect copperplate handwriting and Grandma's scrawl. His were full of jokes and stories, hers were mostly comments on what our mother had told her about us. There were no phone calls, because until late in the war they didn't have a telephone, and long distance calls were expensive anyway.

But once, at least, they came to stay with us. We had all had chickenpox, none of us feeling ill at all, but very itchy. Then unfortunately our mother came down with shingles, which apparently can often be caused by exposure to chickenpox. For once she was really sick, too much for Joyce to handle, together with us three older ones and baby Sarah. So they arrived by train at our little local station, and we were delighted to see them. Grandma, who had previously seemed oblivious to any childish desires, now seemed quite understanding when we wanted to go out and play with our friends, and didn't seem to fuss about our safety as she had before. It must have been autumn. We went out with Grandpa to pick blackberries on the lanes, as we had always done with him before we moved, and we were glad to show him our new home. Howard cried when they left, before and after, and Grandma surprised me again by showing how much she really loved him by the way she talked to him and hugged him. I loved Howard too, and Richard, but I could never show it or tell them — that would have been 'soppy'. It didn't happen until we were adults and not as inhibited. But I was happy that she comforted him.

Coming to the End

In April 1943 I became ten years old. The war was still going on, but the worst parts seemed to have diminished for the moment. Partly this was because the air raids occurred mostly in daylight, and even though they were frequent this was much less scary. They could even be exciting! Once when we were playing on the swing a German plane came zooming in above our house, almost down to chimney level– no warning siren, just literally out of the blue. We could even see the pilot. This, of course, was something we could enlarge upon to our friends — "We could see the Jerry, and you know what, he waved to us!" or similar stories.

That particular plane was aiming at the little bridge over our tiny branch railway. It didn't damage the bridge, but strafed the road and the people on it, then went on and dropped a solitary bomb. Nineteen people altogether were killed in that small raid, but I do not remember anyone telling us that at the time. We were still being protected. Or perhaps, now that I read the newspapers avidly and listened to the news on the radio I had become used to the idea that people died. If we didn't know them it made no difference to us.

It wasn't that I was no longer scared. I still prayed every night that the war would end soon. If we went to the cinema, a rare occurrence, I made sure I was not sitting under a chandelier. I had read in the paper about someone being killed when an explosion shook the building so much one fell down on her. I avoided the newsreels that came before every movie, with their screaming dive bombers and shattered towns. Oddly enough, our own little town, with its own share of bomb damage, didn't bother me as much. I got used to it.

And for those who think the London Blitz was the only episode of German bombing in the war, Exmouth was a good example of how wrong they are. The raids there were completely indiscriminate, and largely without warning. They killed more people than I ever knew at the time. I don't know its exact population at the beginning of the war, but I doubt if it could have been more than 12,000. It was easy to walk from one side to the other in any direction, and we lived right on its eastern edge. There was some bomb damage in every part of it, and people died all over, just carrying on their everyday activities. And it was the same for every town and village, every farm and building, on the South Coast of England.

Before we arrived there, in January 1941, Chapel Street, the narrow little street with our toyshop in it, was hit by three high explosive bombs. Nine adults and three children lost their lives. March 1, 1941 — Three houses destroyed, six adults and three children killed; February 12, 1942, 8 am, three bombs in a residential area — Five deaths, seven injuries; February 26, 1943, mid-day, eight bombs in town center, twenty five killed, forty injured.

These were typical. There were many more raids and deaths. Sometimes people died in canon or machine gun fire as pilots chased them along streets. Sometimes, they were victims of one plane that would drop one bomb then go on and shoot up another area, like one casualty of the February 26 raid, a man working in his garden allotment who was killed this way, All the deaths in the dozens of raids were civilians, many of them children.

On a spring day in 1943 my mother and I went downtown to buy me some new shoes. I was growing fast and even my mother agreed that my old ones were too tight. We went first to the shop where we always bought our shoes, a small family owned store on the main square known as "The Strand". There were several adjoining shops there, with a bus stop outside. The Strand looked pretty that day; it had an above ground brick air raid shelter in it, but the lawns were maintained and there were daffodils in the flower beds. And it was a fine, sunny day.

We knew the owners of the shoe shop, and they knew us. But that didn't help when my mother discovered she had forgotten my clothing coupons. They couldn't sell us a thing without those coupons. So we went out into the sunlight and walked across the flowery square, intending to buy a new record of "Run, Rabbit, Run" at the music shop there. Our old record had finally been dropped and shattered.

We'd just gone into the music shop and greeted the attendant when there was a roar and a huge explosion. The building shook, the windows rattled. The attendant grabbed me and threw me under the stairs, then threw himself on top of me. My mother fell on the floor. Plaster dropped from the ceiling. A silence, then cries, shouting, bells — engines starting up. The attendant pulled himself off me, my mother pushed herself up from the floor.

"That was close!" said the attendant. My mother called a taxi, and it came. Perhaps it was the one driven by the aunt of Margot Fonteyn, the famous ballerina, who was a taxi driver there during the war. As we left the Strand, my mother said "Don't look, darling". But I'd already seen the pile of rubble that was the remains of our shoe shop and the other little shops, and the weirdly bent bus that had been standing outside. It was the bus we might have taken to Littleham and home.

That was the raid of February 26, 1943 — Exmouth's worst raid in the war, the one where more people were killed than in any other, including our shoe shop owners and all the people in the bus outside.

Strangely, I don't think that experience affected me nearly as much as the earlier night raids when we were in Portsmouth. My mother, of course, said little about it. I expect she was really more shaken than I was. But I do know I told nobody about it, and asked no questions. It wasn't until much later that I knew that the shoe shop owners had been killed, though I must have suspected it. And life went on as usual — no further restrictions, no more warnings. Because, after all, what could one do about it? Only winning the war could make things safer.

Hunting spies was now out; there was no more spy hysteria by 1943. The British internees, often Jewish refugees from Nazi Germany themselves, had long been released from internment camps and were occupied in the war effort themselves. We were no longer worried about invasion, but the church bells still didn't ring on Sundays, or any other time. The barbed wire on the cliffs, the concrete blocks on the beaches intended to deter tanks were still there. And rationing, of almost every-thing, was even stricter.

But even though I was less scared by air raids and was enjoying so much about our new lives, winning the war became an obsession of mine. I followed the course of it devotedly. I had always loved Geography and maps. For Christmas 1943 I received an atlas — not a pretty one or a children's edition, but a regular, boring looking cloth bound volume. I could not have been happier. Now I could see what was happening in Russia or Italy, understand why it was so easy for German planes to nip across the channel and bomb us.

I had already enthusiastically painted posters at school encouraging people to support the brave Russian people. These mainly involved images of a British lion and a sturdy Russian bear embracing affectionately. I assume this was part of some government sponsored campaign intended to booster patriotism and support of our new ally, previously an enemy. I don't know what happened to those posters, but I doubt if they had much affect on the British public.

When we were told that our Uncle Jimmy, the oldest of our father's brothers, was coming to visit, we were really excited. He was in the Tank Corps, and had been helping to entertain the troops with his acting skills. We seldom met anyone in the armed forces who had actually been on active service, because they were all abroad fighting. So we awaited him eagerly, both as a link to our father and as a real soldier. I organized the boys into singing patriotic songs for him, and we practiced saluting. Even though he didn't really look like our father he sounded like him. But he didn't stay long, and spent most of his time talking with our mother.

In the evening, however, we all sat on the garden wall in the dark while he told us the names of the stars, planets and galaxies. It was the first I'd heard of the Plow or Orion or the Seven Sisters, and it was the sort of thing our father would have done. So we were happy.

Men!

We were lucky that we did have men in our lives. We weren't the only children who didn't see their fathers the whole of the war. Many didn't have uncles or grandfathers nearby either. When their fathers came home they were often different, and the children hardly knew them. Our relatives weren't always there, but we did sometimes see them. And there were other casual acquaintances.

There were regular ones, like Mr. Norman, who delivered our groceries from Hoopers, the grocery in Budleigh. Although we were closer to Exmouth and its shops, Hoopers was much better than anything in Exmouth, so my mother liked shopping there. She'd either phone in a list or we'd go over and she'd stand at the counter and make her wishes known. Since everyone there seemed to like her — the pretty young widow with four children who talked to all the staff and knew their names — she was sometimes offered, in a few words spoken surreptitiously over the counter, some item in short supply that had just unexpectedly come in. So even though, unlike those who had possessed the means to stock up and hoard scarce foods at the beginning of the war, she never had anything stored away, we had occasional luxuries. Icing sugar, raisins, a few extra eggs — all these sometimes found their way into our house, without any extra cash being spent — or no more than she would normally spend on such purchases. And the person who delivered all these was Mr. Norman — always addressed and referred to this way even though at the time he was just a 'delivery boy'. We all knew him, we all talked to him. He was a real Devon lad, friendly and straightforward, not in the least concerned with being a different 'class' than we were.

After the war he went on and founded his own small chain of supermarkets, the first in the area. He became a multimillionaire, and owned a lovely Georgian mansion looking down on the Exe Estuary. We were all delighted.

Our part time gardener, old Gatter, who worked for us the first year or so we were in Exmouth, was different again. He also came from an ancient local family. He was small, ruddy complexioned and bent from too much bending and stooping. We could barely understand his speech — it was the broadest dialect possible, seldom heard any more. It contained odd words inherited probably from foreign seamen washed up on the rugged Devon coast — words like 'desabillies', which meant underwear, and could be traced back to the French word 'deshabilles'. 'er were bowerly' meant 'She was a pretty woman.' An old man was a 'gatfer' or 'gaffer'', a dozen was a 'dizzen' — there were so many words that we didn't understand. But in the end we did, and Gatter's stories about pirate's caves along our coast and Spanish doubloons found, apparently, in all of them, inspired many of our expeditions of discovery (or lack of it).

We were not completely cut off from the Royal Marines, because there was a long established training camp in close by Lympstone, and a temporary wartime camp in Dalditch Common, a large area of heathland above Budleigh. Some of the officers had known my father, and our mother was occasionally invited to functions at Lympstone. I only remember her going to one, and I remember being excited for her that she was going to a party. But she came back a little sad. She had been assigned to a young officer, and he apparently had been shy and uneasy in his task of looking after her. Obviously for once she had failed to charm — or had simply found the situation too difficult emotionally.

But the other occasion, which we children all remember, was much more successful. We were invited by a certain Major Clelland, who had, I think, known our father, to an afternoon at the camp on Dalditch. There was a fabulous tea set out for us in the prefab. Officers' Mess — sandwiches, cakes, cookies, even candy, tea from big urns which tasted funny but good. We ate all we could, and then we had a real adventure. Dalditch was a place where the troops did manoeuvres in tanks and other vehicles, testing them and themselves for battle in rugged territory. We were all, even Sarah, I think, taken for a ride in a 'Bren gun carrier'. This was a small armored tracked vehicle, used for transporting personnel and machine guns during the War. We hurtled down into gullies, up over steep ridges, over bushes and ditches, through streams and muddy lanes. It was wonderful, one of the best rides of my life — all done with no seat belts, no restraints of any sort — just the assumption that we were sensible people who knew how to look after ourselves and didn't want to die!

It confirmed our opinion of the Royal Marines, the bravest and the best of all the Services, the one we still felt was ours.

As Sarah grew up and started to talk she must have become aware that other children had men that they called 'Daddy'. Sometimes, if we were with one of our elderly neighbors, or anyone else's father, she would try out the word, and call him 'Daddy'. Even then, it seemed so sad to me, but also embarrassing. I don't know what was said to her, but in time she stopped, and as far as I can remember never used the word again.

Suddenly at the end of 1943 there were plenty of young men around. One morning the boys and I went off to play in the fields opposite. By the five barred gate that we climbed to get in there was a strange look-ing sentry, and beyond him, all over our fields, were khaki tents and soldiers in baggy uniforms moving around. We gazed in amazement. "Hi kids!" said the sentry. "Want any gum?" — and we realized, be-cause of course we recognized American (Yankee) accents, that they were Americans, our allies. And of course we wanted gum, though we'd never had any before, because my mother didn't allow it.

That gum — 'Juicy Fruit', peppermint, spearmint — and all the candies, so different from ours — we lived on them that winter. Of course our mother objected, but what could she do? They showered us with them whenever they saw us. I think they thought we were starv-ing — they were very young, mostly farm boys from the Mid West, far from home and looking for friends. Their huge, noisy trucks broke down our sidewalks and lampposts, roared down our quiet roads. We didn't mind. Loaded with young men singing "Deep in the heart of Texas" or "Roll out the barrel', they flung handfuls of candy wherever they went. We discovered that if we stationed our little blonde sister on the street she would collect even more candy, ("Hi Blondie!"), and we'd collect it from her later. I went to school chewing it, and had a special place on a wall where I hid it before I went in to school, so I could pick it up afterwards.

We were madly envious of friends who had officers billeted on them, like my friend Dorks. Her mother had space in her house, and they had two young men living with them for the whole winter. Dorks and her mother loved them both, and kept in touch with the one who survived the war. We, of course, had a full house already — no chance of getting some ourselves. But surveys after the war showed that the American soldiers sent to Devon, both black and white, found it a warm, friendly place. The hope that they brought, their youth and vulnerability, made them welcome everywhere.

Books

I was always running out of books. By the time I was eleven I'd gone through just about all the children's books in Boots' lending library. Hythe House School didn't have a library, or if they did it was so minimal I've forgotten it. Joyce and Auntie Muriel had plenty of classics, and were willing to lend them to me. There were also a few of Joyce's old books on her shelves, including one I particularly loved, and inherited from her. It was "Martin Pippin in the Apple Orchard" by Eleanor Farjeon — who wrote the poem "Morning has Broken". I read and re-read that book. Now it seems very dated and sexist, but then I found it magical, and about the only story resembling fantasy that I really enjoyed. Perhaps it was the language, which drew one into a different, very beautiful world.

I borrowed books wherever I could find them. One source was a lady who lived in a house on the main road, just opposite the Broadway, our street. I don't know how we knew her. The house always looked closed up, the lady never seemed to come out. But somehow I was invited in to look through her son's books. It was all quiet inside, very different from our house. Her son had been killed earlier on in the war. There did not seem to be anyone else in the family.

His books were all typical boys' books — annuals, adventure stories, school stories — no classics, no Arthur Ransome. But I had my own Arthur Ransomes — I saved all my money for each one as it came out. And I liked boys' books better than girls' books. So I read every one her son had left. And she was happy to let me do it.

When the end of the war came her house was the only one not draped in flags. It still had the curtains drawn tight. My mother disapproved. She said that everybody had someone to mourn — peace was something to celebrate in any case. But I still felt sorry for the lady, all alone in that silent house.

The best way to keep up with my reading, I found, was to take books I had been sent for Christmas and birthdays, but did not really enjoy, down to Elands, the bookshop in Exmouth, close to where the shoe shop had been. Fortunately it had not been damaged. It was a small shop, 500 square feet at the most, and filled with my favorites as well as all the new titles.

I had always used my gift certificates and money gifts there. I discovered that they would buy back books from me, if they were fairly new and didn't have my name in them. Then I could prowl the store blissfully, pick up books and read as much as I had time for, discover whether I liked them enough to buy them. The staff soon got to know me, and were very helpful and kind. I think they probably bought books they didn't really need from me. When I became a bookseller myself I realized how delightful it is to discover a child who really adores reading, and I usually tried to help children who couldn't afford the books they longed for.

Shopping on my own, going downtown, had become easier in 1943, because I had finally saved up enough to buy my bike. Bikes were hard to get — one had to order them and then wait weeks. Waiting was awful — I kept going into the bike shop and asking when it was coming. I came to love the exciting smell of rubber tires, and it still brings back that store, and my impatience.

When it actually arrived it certainly wasn't the glamorous sort of bike kids have now. I had to buy the cheapest. A Raleigh, the brand meant to be best, was far too expensive. My bike was a Hercules, dull black all over to prevent any shiny surface from reflecting light and attracting enemy bombers. It had wooden pedals, because rubber was in short supply and 'needed for the war effort'. But I loved it, and thought it the most beautiful bike in the world. We bought a basket for it, so that I could carry my books to school, and my swim suit and towel if we went to the beach, or anything else I might need. And soon after, acting on her desire to make sure that we all had the same, my mother found second hand bikes for Howard and Richard, so we were all equipped to go off on expeditions together.

I had enjoyed being ten so much that I remember thinking it would be nice to remain that age forever. Being eleven was pretty good too, but it was the beginning of growing up, and some of that was not very welcome. I suppose it began when my mother told me I was 'too big' to have baths with my brothers, That was probably literally true — we were a tighter and tighter fit, and Richard was beginning to object to sitting 'under the drips'. But there was something about my mother's voice that told me that there was more to it than my size. It was the same when she said that this summer "You really need to wear a 'vest' (English term for undershirt) under your shirt".

I had a nasty feeling that this had to do with the unwelcome protuberances that were appearing on my chest. These meant 'growing up' — something I had decided I did not want to do. It wasn't that I really minded being a girl. In lots of ways I quite liked it. I enjoyed wearing pretty dresses, and even now, when getting a new one was virtually impossible, I was lucky enough to inherit one occasionally from a distant cousin. I actually thought I was quite pretty, though my brothers tried hard to persuade me of the opposite — "Look, her nose almost touches her chin!" "See what tiny little eyes she has!" But I still found large groups of girls scary and didn't know how to fit in.

What I did not like was the assumption that girls could not do certain things. My brothers assumed I couldn't make model planes, which every small boy did during the war. So I made my own. But I found it boring and didn't continue. When I went for a ride on the coal man's truck or climbed a cliff the other mothers would cluck disapprovingly because "Girls don't do things like that!" Some other girls did climb trees occasionally, but didn't wiggle along a stream as it passed through a culvert under a lane, or build huts or have battles. They, like their mothers, seemed to think that some activities were reserved for boys.

But the compensation was that boys liked me — not as a girl, but just as a friend. I felt honored when two slightly older boys who had built a really elaborate, partly underground hut, invited me to go over and join them in it. There was nothing sexy about it — we were just comrades who enjoyed doing the same things.

In fact sex in any form had never entered my life or even my imagination, and I didn't want it to. But inevitably it did, at least as far as information went. Of course there were those small breasts, which I hated. Then one day at school, as we were putting our tennis racquets into their cases after a game, the other girls began to talk about something mysterious, referred to as 'starting'. One of the bigger girls had

just 'started' and the others were full of curiosity. "Does it hurt?".
"How long does it last?" "Do your brothers know about it?".

They seemed to know at least what it was. I didn't. So I asked —
and was greeted with amazement and ridicule. "She doesn't know what
a period is!" "And I thought she knew everything!" "How weird she
is!" So they proceeded to tell me, in full and gory detail.

I decided this was not going to happen to me. How could people put
up with it? No swimming, no bike riding, no sports at school? Cramps
and mess and not being able to talk about it? How could anyone survive
being a girl? As far as I could, I put it out of my mind. The last thing I
considered was asking my mother about it — but in fact she did try to
tell me some time later. She was so embarrassed that all she could say
about menstruation was "It happens once a month, and it means you
can have babies". This was hardly reassuring! But I soon discovered
that other girls did seem to do a lot of the things that my schoolmates
had warned me were banned, so my fears diminished.

And I had some help in my need to learn more. There was another
influx of evacuees from the London area when the Germans started
to attack that part of Britain with 'Flying bombs' — the V1 and V2
rockets that caused at least 9000 deaths in the autumn of 1944 and the
spring of '45. These were particularly terrifying, especially the V2s, for
which there was no warning and no defense.

We and the rest of Britain were too far away to be subjected to this
horror, but many parents in that area sent their children to safer places.
For a while, till the Allies reached the Nazi launching pads, I had something else to dread.

The Pratts next door took in one girl of about my age — Jean Rees,
her name was. We awaited her eagerly, preparing to make her a mem-
ber of our "Cormorant Club". I don't think she stayed long, and I don't
think she really became one of our gang, but she was pleasant enough,
and she and I got on well. It was nice to have a girl next door for a
change, and it was much easier to get to know her since we were always 'one on one'. It was the first time I'd enjoyed gossiping with a
girl, and we'd sit in the overhang of our garden shed and discuss things
of interest to us both. One of these turned out to be sex, and for the
first time I really got the basic story. I actually learned how babies are
made — and "Don't do it with your brothers!" she warned me. The

172

whole thing sounded amazing and unlikely, but at least not scary as she described it.

My mother had her suspicions about our conversations. She didn't approve of Jean, who disappeared from my life soon after. But Jean's information was the most I ever received until I started reading about the process myself much later. For some reason it never occurred to me to do that then, though I did find that certain passages in my mother's books (generally forbidden to me) became much more explicable.

There was too much else going on in my life for worries about growing up to be a major concern. In fact I was growing up in other ways. This was the year that I became aware that even children could do things that helped other people. I was still nominally at least a Brownie, and before Christmas 1943 our 'Brown Owl', the formidable Mrs. Murray, took us to a local 'Old Peoples' Home' and we sang carols to them. Of course I knew many old people, and I had seen my mother take meals over to an old couple who were caretaking the house opposite, but it had never occurred to me that we could do anything for them ourselves. The old people in the Home loved us. We could see their faces brighten up, and some of them sang with us. They persuaded us to go on and on singing, then wanted us to stay and talk with them. But Mrs. Murray thought it was getting too near bedtime.

My mother was a good example of someone who did a lot of good without belonging to any group, or making a big deal out of it. The couple across the street were just one example. He had been a gardener, but was now too old. She had serious rheumatoid arthritis and was confined to a wheelchair. My mother would bring her over to have tea with us in the garden, and regularly visited them, even managing to keep some chicken and Christmas pudding from our Christmas dinner to take over to them. That must have been hard to do, since we were always so hungry and didn't often get chicken, which was a luxury in those days. But my mother found many others to help in small ways. Eggs were in short supply but when my old art teacher Mr. Lambert was ill she sent me over with some eggs for him.

That should have been a learning experience for me, because it once more introduced me to a death. When Mrs. Lambert opened the door to me it was to tell me that Mr. Lambert had died the day before. Standing there with the eggs in my hand, I had no idea what to say. She called me 'dear' and looked worried, but I could offer her no comfort. Since death was never mentioned in our home, and hugs had been few for quite a long time, it did not occur to me even to say I was sorry. I fled home, to tell my mother briefly "He died", and disappeared to my books.

I didn't see Mrs. Lambert again, and my mother never talked to me about the incident. Mr. Lambert had left me a beautiful little pearl brooch that had belonged to his mother, and I have treasured it ever since. I heard a friend of my mother's ask her how I had reacted, and my mother's "Oh, she didn't say much." I knew I had not done enough, but it wasn't until years later, until well into adulthood, that I began to discover how to express sympathy.

I went on painting, but I really missed the friendly criticism that Mr. Lambert had provided. It wasn't enough to be told by a teacher at school that a painting of mine was very good, because I didn't know whether she herself knew enough to judge. Mr. Lambert was a good painter himself, and I trusted him.

But 1944 was a year when the good outweighed the bad. One morning we discovered that our field was now empty again. Flattened grasses, a few abandoned tent pegs, these were all that remained. Our 'Yanks' had disappeared overnight — and we knew they had gone off to fight. We had a good idea also of where they would be fighting. For a long time we had seen landing barges in bays and coves along the coast. The trucks full of singing troops had always been making for our beaches. Now the barges were gone too. It would be an invasion.

And then one night I awoke to hear the air filled with the constant roar of aircraft. It had a friendly sound — there were no engines with the tell tale German thumping rhythm — and it went on all night. We knew what it was. We had seen planes towing the huge black gliders on practice expeditions — we knew they were for carrying troops into battle. And I was filled with hope.

I followed the Normandy invasion day by day. The radio and the Daily Telegraph told the story of victories and some setbacks. Much more was made of the victories. I made a map of Europe, and marked Allied advances in red crayon. Finally it looked as if the war might be coming to an end. The Nazis were being chased!

In an attempt to do something real for 'the war effort' I gathered my 'gang' otherwise known as 'the Cormorant Club' and planned a money

174

raising effort for 'Salute the Soldier' week. There were seven of us by then, myself, Hugh and Bobby Pratt, Howard, Richard and Sarah, and a boy called John Bailey. He was a nice boy with a triangular smile, and usually he wanted to play 'wild animals' — African ones — because he had grown up there. He and his little sister were living with their grandparents up the street and their parents were in Kenya. It seemed strange that they should be in Exmouth, not with them, since it was much safer in Kenya.

Our ages ranged from four to eleven.

The first need was for something to sell. I ordained that we should each make something. Sarah was exempted from this requirement. I made small dolls out of straw and scraps of fabric, threading yarn through the straw to make hair. The boys made mostly small model planes out of scraps from their building kits. And I had just discovered how to make whistles out of hollowed out laurel twigs — they actually worked, so I included some of these. Then there were flowers from our gardens, and drawings by some of us — the boys' almost all of planes, and mine of sail boats.

When 'Salute the Soldier' week started we set out with our trays of motley small objects, and toured the neighborhood knocking on doors. Our prices were low. I do not think our mothers knew what we were doing. For whatever reason, almost everybody bought something. Perhaps we looked rather pathetic, with our somewhat unattractive wares. In any case, we raised what to us was a sizeable amount of money. This we delivered to our mother, who did not criticize, but took it off to the relevant organization.

She returned irate. The official collecting the money had told her that he could not take it, because we had been selling our miserable items! This was illegal for juveniles. Needless to say, she had made a big fuss, and eventually he accepted it. A week later, in a list of donations published by the Exmouth Journal, the following appeared "Miss Susan Hayter 15 shillings from a collection among friends". It was the first time I received a mention in the press. At last I felt I was doing something to help end the war!

The other thing we did was later in the war, after the Netherlands was liberated. So many Dutch people needed clothes and food after their terrible 'Hunger Winter' when the Germans cut off their food supplies and up to 22,000 people died. The Fergusons, the Dutch refugees down our street, and our mother, who had such happy memories of Holland, were particularly concerned about this. This time I think we had some adult direction in our efforts to help. I do know that Eric Ferguson joined us for the first time. Again we traveled the neighborhood, picking up cans of food and clothing for the Dutch, and transporting them in wheelbarrows back to Eric's house. Some of the cans were really old, and so were the clothes. I remember some moth eaten woolen long johns, with holes all over them, and I wondered if anyone would want them, however cold it was. I hated to be cold — I was glad to help the poor Dutch.

And it was cold that winter, 1944 to '45, one of the coldest in Western Europe's history. Even in Devon, with a mild climate that allows palm trees to grow on the coast, we had snow, and for us, unlike the Dutch, it was wonderful! The whole of Devon is up and down — there is very little flat land. We had small hills all around us. One of them we had christened "Cormorant Hill' and considered it our club's territory. The hill certainly wasn't ideal for sledding. There were large mole hills all over it, and at the bottom of the steepest slope there was a stream. The hill was covered with snow that was only a few inches deep. That was enough for us.

At first we tried with trays from home, but they didn't slide too well. Then, having observed some other children using pieces of corrugated iron bent up in the front and shooting down the hill on them, we somehow managed to acquire the same. My mother was doubtful. This would obviously be a dangerous procedure, with the up turned end of the metal sheet ready to pierce us if we fell on top of it. But she let us do it. So off we went, in our everyday clothes, gray flannel shorts for the boys, a skirt and knee socks for me, woolen school coats on top, rubber boots below, and had one of the most blissful days of our lives. Sarah, of course, was left behind. She was certainly safer that way!

The sky was a clear blue, and for the first time I noticed how it acquired a different, yellowish tint against the brilliant white snow. It was still quite cold. The snow squeaked a little when one walked on it. We positioned our 'sled' on the top of Cormorant Hill, and the three of us piled on. Then, our hands pushing off at the sides, we were off — hurtling downhill towards the stream, missing the mole hills, only managing to stop just in time to miss the icy stream. Over and over we did it, avoiding the mole hills each time, though we watched other kids flying into the air as they collided with one.

The next day it was all over. We went up to the hill, but there were bare patches, and the snow wasn't slippery any more. Devon's balmy weather had returned. But that one day was as exciting as any visit to the Alps could ever be.

We did not, of course, think of the children in Germany, where British and American bombing was far more pervasive and destructive than anything had been in Britain. We were just children, enjoying a childhood that in its way was more free than anything that came after.

Our Favorite Place

April, 1944 — D-Day was yet to come, but another thing happened to us all in that month — much less world shaking, but to us children more immediately important, and long lasting in its effects. We went to Rogues' Roost for the first time.

It was Mrs. Murray, our doctor's wife and my Brownie leader, who was responsible for this. She called my mother one day, and asked if I could go with their family to a farm guesthouse on Dartmoor, the great stretch of wild moorland that lay to the west of the Exe estuary.

I think my mother must have been torn by this request. We had not had a vacation since the two weeks in the Isle of Wight, four years ago. Was it fair that I should have this opportunity, and not the boys? She asked if I would like to go. Of course I would. I liked Shirley Murray, a friendly blonde girl of my age, and I had longed to go to Dartmoor, the nearest piece of countryside that resembled the Lake District in the Arthur Ransome books. But my answer put my mother in a quandary. What could she do for the boys? And perhaps she also felt "What about me?" For surely she must have needed a vacation more than any of us.

And, I realize, she might have worried about me, because I had never been away without her, had never even had a 'sleepover' at a friend's house. So there were incentives for what she did — which did, in a way, detract just a little from the excitement I felt.

She decided that the whole family, including Joyce, would go to Rogues' Roost too, if there was room there. And there was. I would still be Shirley's guest, and would share a room with her. My family would just be there too.

I have no idea how this worked out for the adults. My mother had nothing in common with Mrs. Murray, and I don't know how she afforded it. Though I did learn later that on subsequent visits she was given a discount as a war widow. But for me, and I think for my brothers, this was the start of a love affair — a love affair with a place, a place we have all, including Sarah, gone back to again and again, finding its magic so strong that we can feel again exactly as we did as children.

Howard and Richard both went there on their honeymoons. Sarah, on her trips back from Denmark with husband and children, would make straight for Dartmoor, leaving husband Jorgen complaining that he never got to see London. I too go back whenever I get the chance, though now partially to clean and oil the teak memorial bench that Howard, Richard and I put up for Sarah in the churchyard at Leusdon. As children at Rogue's Roost we sometimes went to church there, more willingly than we ever went to the Littleham church at home.

It was difficult — and fun — to get to Rogue's Roost. This was a large farmhouse in the midst of the moor, at least twelve miles from any form of public transport. And those twelve miles are on tiny lanes and narrow bridges (narrow means about one car wide), up and down steep hills. But the journey started way before that.

First we took the local taxi to Exmouth harbor. Then, the first excitement, we embarked on one of the ancient ferries that crossed the Exe Estuary to Starcross, a tiny town on the far side. Down the rickety steps to the little ship, close to the green seaweed draping the timbers of the dock, onto the open deck and wooden benches. The captain sounded the horn for departure. We clung to the railings as the harbor disappeared behind us, through the gap in the barbed wire barrier that was meant to deter invaders, into the open waters of the estuary. Seagulls wheeled overhead, the wake frothed out behind us.

On the far shore we could see two white boats built to look like swans, and each journey after that we watched for them. At the wooden jetty there was even a porter waiting, an old man who helped my mother and Joyce carry the luggage to the platform. There we waited until the little 'Puffing Billy' drew up. The guard's whistle blew, the engine let out a wheeze and gradually started puffing black smoke, and we were off.

The journey, very short, was and is one of the prettiest in England. It follows the shore almost all the way, passing through tunnels in the red clay cliffs, coming out to views of sparkling sea and little hilly towns, brilliant green meadows and dark red cows, harbors and sail boats. It was not long enough for us. We went through Teignmouth, a small port from which my New Zealand cousin Adrian would later set sail on a solo voyage to his far off country. This had been the first town in Devon to be bombed, at the station where we stopped for a minute. Recently I met a woman whose parents had died in that raid.

At Newton Abbot a taxi was waiting. The driver was a gray haired lady called Mrs. French. She lived near Rogues' Roost, and met us every time we went there. We were on the last leg of our journey, and the best. We skirted the little granite town of Ashburton, turning onto a narrow road that wound above the town and onto a ridge, old houses with big shady gardens on each side, paddocks with grazing horses, gray stone walls with little plants growing out of them. Gradually there were fewer and fewer houses; the road descended into a deep valley with mossy woods. A small river flowed through it, the water clear and brown, cascading over granite rocks.

We crossed the river twice, on two ancient bridges just wide enough for one car, then left it and climbed until the trees disappeared and we were in a wide open space, cropped lawn like grass, a couple of shaggy ponies grazing, a small rocky stream winding through it. High hills covered in gorse and heather rose on each side — and we went on, higher and higher, until we could see more hills in every direction, some of them crowned with granite peaks.

"What's that?" I asked Mrs. French., pointing at one of the highest. "Oh, that's Buckland Beacon, love"

I knew about beacons — hills where bonfires had been lit in times of peril, when foes had been sighted, or in celebration, such as a Coronation. A fire had probably been lit at Buckland Beacon when the Spanish Armada was sighted off Plymouth, not so far away.

Seeing those hills, breathing the scent of the moor, I thought for the first time in my life "This is my kind of country". And it still is.

In the midst of this country, with its own surrounding hills, its own tiny rushing stream, was Rogues' Roost. We came over a high rise, with tors (the granite outcroppings I'd seen) on each side of us, and looked down on the tiny hamlet called Sheril. The lane was directly onto the moor — no fences, walls or hedges — just a vista of rolling hills in every direction, surrounding and enfolding the four or five houses there.

And silence — no traffic, no planes, just an occasional bleat from one of the new lambs playing near their grazing mothers.

Mrs. French stopped the car. "That's Rogues Roost" She pointed down at the largest house in the hamlet.

It was a large, gray, E shaped house, with its front covered with ivy. The center of the E faced in our direction. Behind it was another small building, and a barn or cow shed. Up the hill a little way was another, more modern house, looking down the hill.

In our direction, to our left, there were two dwellings — one an ancient Devon farmhouse, thatched and sprawling, built of granite in the medieval long house pattern, animals at one end, people at the other. A farmyard and farm buildings surrounded it. And this side of it was a small cottage with a shed behind it and washing strung on a line.

Opposite these houses was a tall stone house with church like windows. "They call it 'Hornet's Castle'," Mrs. French said.

In time we knew all of the people who lived in those houses. For now, Mrs. French started the car, and we rolled down the hill towards Rogues' Roost.

We only spent a week there that first time but its impact on us was as strong as the three months we'd spent in Rochester in 1940.

The house itself took the place of a much earlier one with a sinister reputation of some sort — madness, murder? — hence the name. This one had been built about 1900. It felt older, with its Elizabethan era plan and ivy covered walls. But there was nothing 'pseudo' about it — it was a plain, simple, if rather large, farmhouse. As you walked in the door there was a typical English country porch, raincoats hanging from hooks, muddy boots on the floor, an umbrella rack.

Another door, then a hall, with a staircase rising to the right. On the wall to the right of the stairs were a set of prints. They showed people in the costumes of some foreign country, and one of them had round eyes rather like Richard's — or so we thought. We sometimes called him 'fish eyes'. That became one of the familiar objects that greeted us each time we went.

There was a sitting room to the left and another next to it. I think the first was 'adults only', because I don't remember using it. In the other there were two life size one dimensional wooden figures, one male, one female, clad in old time clothes. Later, on one rainy day, our mother draped some wet clothes on them, and earned the only reprimand I ever remember at Rogues' Roost. They were apparently priceless antiques!

To the right of the front door was the dining room, with tables for each family group. There we had wonderful meals — foods we had forgotten existed — real scrambled eggs, from the farm's own chickens, not from horrible dried eggs; puddings with cream, unseen for years; freshly baked bread and home made jam, from real fruit. Nothing has ever been more delicious.

Upstairs were numerous bedrooms, one 'loo', and one bathroom. Bath time — required for us children — had to be scheduled carefully, not just because there were a lot of people to fit in, but because one had to be careful that the hot water didn't run out. I think we managed our obligatory bath each evening. I remember the hot, steamy, green painted room with its huge old fashioned bath tub — fortunately still big enough for the three of us older ones. I was allowed to bath with my brothers just for this week.

Shirley and I shared a room on the corner of the house, looking both up and down the hill. Like almost all the rooms, it had wide window seats, and on those seats Shirley and I would curl up together under one of our quilts in the morning and talk. I do not remember one word of what we talked about, but I do remember what fun it was, and how much it added to all the other pleasures of the trip. It's associated in my mind with my first pajamas, exciting in themselves, because I had never had pajamas before, and knew that most girls wore them. I had worn nighties, because my mother liked little girls in feminine clothes, even though she didn't mind my unfeminine activities. I had begged her for pajamas as soon as she decided I could go with the Murrays, and finally she had given way, and bought me some boys' flannel ones with stripes and a draw string waist. I was delighted with them.

For that week, although we children all did things together, I was mostly with Shirley and her family, a situation which worked quite well for me. There was so much to do and explore, so many new people and places and experiences. Our various visits all blend together in my mind, but there are some that I know belong to that first occasion.

Our first day, a bright, blustery spring morning, we children were all turned loose after breakfast and started to explore. It was chilly — I was wearing a blue sweater that I'd recently received in our first (and only) CARE package from America. I loved it because of the color, and because it was new, but it was rather itchy wool, and a bit too tight. New clothes were rare — I wasn't going to complain.

We followed the lane that led down the hill, next to the little stream that flowed beside it. Hills rose on each side of us, the lower slopes divided into small fields by dry stone walls made of enormous granite slabs. Some of the fields were newly plowed and dark brown, others green, with a few cows or horses. The grass between us and the stream was lawn like, velvety, cropped by the sheep that wandered freely everywhere. Granite rocks lay scattered, punctuating the flow of the stream. And at the bottom of the hill, where the stream joined its much larger neighbor, the Walla Brook, there was a wider lawn, with small, shaggy ponies grazing on it. They looked up as we approached, hoping to pet them, but as soon as we got closer they wheeled and trotted up into the heather and gorse that surrounded the 'lawn'. They were wild ponies, free to roam the moor, some of the few wild horses left in Britain.

We were all wearing our rubber boots, so the Walla Brook was too tempting. Clear and brown from the peaty soil, it rushed along, over rocks, under overhanging branches and shrubs. There was a bridge over it, but why take the bridge when one could wade? We plunged in, soon discovering that the water was deeper than expected, and went over the tops of our boots. Richard, being smaller, was wet up to his thighs. On the other side we made our way back to the bridge, and hung our wet socks on the rail, then continued our explorations.

I had never been anywhere so quiet and deserted. No traffic, no human sounds, nothing but the wind in the trees, the chatter of the little river, the baaing of sheep on the hillside. I longed to be alone in it, and sometimes later I could be. I would go up the hill above the house where there was an old abandoned quarry, now all grass and heather. I would repeat to myself "Nobody can see me, nobody can hear me" and it was the most liberating feeling in my life. Even here, though, there was a reminder of the war. One day, blown in the breeze, I heard the faint wailing of a far off air raid siren. There was no fear in it — it was too remote, too dreamlike. Perhaps I even imagined it.

But this visit had plenty of its own pleasures. This was our introduction, a voyage of discovery. We met for the first time the person we called "Ronnie' — Miss Veronica Cave-Penney, the owner of the farm, child of the people who built the house. She was tall and quiet, with very short grey hair "almost like a man!" my mother remarked — and always wore trousers, except on Sundays, when she would go off to her duties as Church Warden at Leusdon Church wearing a pale blue outfit. "Ronnie looks so pretty in a dress!" my mother would regularly remark, in contrast to her general disapproval of trousers.

We were a little in awe of Ronnie that first time — she didn't appear much in the house, being a genuine farmer, and busy most of the time with crops or animals. But the next time, and those after, Ronnie became a lifelong friend. She watched patiently as we tried riding the partly wild pony Penrose, who was out on the moor all winter. She listened as we told her about our other lives, and she told us a lot about the moor and the places and people on it. She instructed us without seeming to instruct — how to saddle a pony, how to plant a potato, where there were dangerous bogs.

She was one of those women left unmarried by the First World War. Her younger brother Anthony had been killed in the war. A granite cross on the crest of the hill we'd come down memorialized him — a young lieutenant who died 'Gallantly leading his men'. He was nineteen.

Now Ronnie lived in the modern house a short way above the old one. The person who actually ran the guesthouse was Miss Reed, another middle aged woman whose father, we discovered, was warden of the prison in Exeter, a brooding building we could see from Exeter station. She became very fond of Howard and Richard, and invited them to tea at the prison one day. And there was at least one other person who helped in the kitchen — a big job for a farm kitchen, catering for at least fifteen people. There were usually several families and a few solitary fishermen, there to fly fish in the streams and rivers around.

Howard and Richard and I were all fascinated by the farm and wanted to help. I think Shirley was less excited about this, though I don't think she objected when we brought in the cows in the morning for milking, collecting them from their field down the hill and guiding them with sticks and shouts up through the rocks and gorse bushes to the cow shed behind the annex. There Hare, the cowman, would get them settled in their stalls, sit himself down on a stool beside one at a time, and begin to milk them. It was always interesting to watch the milk squirting out of the pink teats, hissing into the metal pail between Hare's knees. I don't remember any particular attention to cleanliness — Hare was always smoking as he milked, and certainly didn't wash his hands. His clothes tended to carry a certain amount of cow dung, and you had to be careful not to slip on it when you walked on the messy, uneven granite floor. But the milk was creamy and delicious, and we never, ever got sick at Rogues' Roost.

It was here that Howard decided that he really wanted to be a farmer. He loved animals of all sorts, and he would have been happy to spend all day with Hare. My mother had decided that Howard would go into the Navy, and when asked what he wanted to do he would hesitantly tell them that was his choice, but it never really was.

There were other animals, pigs, just wandering around the muddy area close to the cow shed, and of course chickens. I remember a pig called Rosie who was not much more than a piglet. She used to come and lean against me, which I found very endearing. A huge old Shire horse called Lion, presumably because of his tawny color, was the 'tractor' of the farm — he did the plowing and any other hauling or carrying work.

On subsequent visits Howard did spend a lot of the time with Hare, who was a kind, gentle man, and seemed to enjoy having us around. I was more interested in exploring the Moor, and particularly in riding. We didn't try it that time, but later I used to ride Penrose, after thirty minutes or so chasing her round the croft with a small pail full of oats before finally catching her. On those rides Penrose had to coaxed all along the outward journey, but on the way home she would take off like the wild pony she was, longing to get me off her back.

We also rode a little black pony called Tiny. Tiny belonged to Peter Hannaford, who lived in the cottage at the entrance to the hamlet. He was an old moors man, who lived with his 'cousin' Ruby (nobody quite knew the relationship) and practiced the farming skills of the past, butchering his own meat, building his own walls, castrating his own sheep, living with no modern conveniences. He probably didn't even have an inside toilet, though I never tried to find out.

I was always a little scared of Peter Hannaford. I think he was perhaps a bit shy, because he wasn't unkind — just very blunt. Ronnie would tell us to go and ask if we could borrow Tiny, and he always said yes, but wasn't too helpful about saddling or bridling her. I never spoke to Ruby — she looked like a gypsy, and was also shy. We were, of course, outsiders — they were real Dartmoor folk, who had probably never been far from home.

My mother must have loved Rogues' Roost too, because we went back again and again. This first time we went for a tea-time picnic down by the Walla Brook, sitting on the soft grassy bank, eating one of those loaves of home made bread with home made butter, and home made jam, tea already mixed with milk in a thermos. My mother, who liked her bread in the form of civilized sandwiches, was not too impressed, but we, deprived at home of fresh bread ("It goes too fast!") all found it wonderful. And Joyce, who also had never been in such empty country, perhaps had never had a holiday, seemed to enjoy every minute of our stay.

We three older children went with the Murrays to Widecombe, the largest and most famous of Dartmoor villages. It held a horse fair once a year, when the wild ponies were rounded up and many of them sold as children's riding horses or pets. They all belonged to various farmers, even though they roamed free on the moor. It also had a beautiful ancient church, and a village green, with numerous granite cottages set around it. It was about three miles each way to walk from Rogue's Roost, and Mrs. Murray had annoyed my mother by banning Sarah from the expedition, thinking she could not walk that far. My mother felt she was the best judge, and also objected to Mrs. Murray's militaristic organization of the trip. Mrs. M. had probably also noticed my mother's habit of wearing high heels to hike in — not something the Girl Guides would have approved!

Widecombe's church was sometimes described as 'the cathedral of the moor' and it had been the after death destination of the local moor dwellers, since there was no other church in that part of the moor. Coffins were carried there on 'coffin roads' — not regular roads but green, grassy paths through the heather and gorse. We followed one of these as far as we could. They weren't maintained, but through centuries of use some stretches survived intact.

There were two high ridges to cross, a valley between them with a stream, small twisted oak trees, and a farm or two. We walked right through one of the farm yards — the farm dogs rushed at us barking, but did us no harm. From each ridge the view expanded — miles of rocky hillsides, on and on to the horizon. It probably was the longest, toughest walk we had ever done, but we had no problems.

We had a picnic lunch on a bench in a square by the church, and went into the beautiful, light filled fourteenth century church afterwards. But then on the same square, we discovered something else, which impressed me just as much, even with my love of old buildings. It was a gift shop in one of the houses by the church.

I had never been into a gift shop. This one was filled with the usual tourist items — small china Dartmoor ponies, plates and cups printed with the famous Widecombe song "Old Uncle Tom Cobbley", maps and postcards and bits of cheap jewelry and fancy pens and pencils, hats and guidebooks — it was all entrancing. There were not many tourists those days on Dartmoor, and some of those items probably dated from before the war. I do remember that a lot of it was covered in dust. I longed to be able to buy something, but of course I didn't have any money.

I longed to go back, and next time I did, persuading my reluctant mother to let me buy one thing. I chose a cheap brooch in the shape of a Dartmoor 'pixy' — but it never looked as good as it had in the gift shop.

It seemed a long way back, but I loved every minute of it. Howard would have preferred to be back on the farm, but he did fine, and so did tough little Richard, now eight and always full of energy. Even Sarah, when we came back in our summer holidays, managed that walk, so Mrs. Murray was wrong, and my mother was right.

Even wet days were fun. Dartmoor is a wet and boggy place. On all occasions when we went to Rogues' Roost there were other children, and a few single people who would join in our games. There were stacks of board games, and shelves full of books I'd never read. And several times one of the fishermen, a stern looking middle aged man, would suddenly come to life, and organize us into a lengthy game of 'Murder", played all over the house. He turned out to be a well known person, W.C. Sellars — Mr. Sellars to us — who was headmaster of Charterhouse, one of the oldest and most prestigious boys' public schools. He was also author of a best selling book "1066 and All That" — a humorous history of England. We became very fond of him, and hoped each visit that he would be there too.

As that first visit came to an end we were sad. When the taxi with Mrs. French reached the top of the hill and we looked back on Rogues' Roost we were in tears. Apparently most visiting children were the same. But luckily my mother found a way to bring us back in August. Joyce went home for a visit to her parents and we took Georgie instead — not quite so much fun because Georgie found Dartmoor too wild and couldn't walk far, but still better than any other place on earth to us children. Ronnie became an important part of our lives, and when she became eighty she confided to me that she had always thought of us as 'her' children. I was moved and honored.

The Waiting Year

We had thought the war would have ended by Christmas 1944. D Day, and the swift advances through France, had made us all optimistic. My map showed the allies gradually winning. But in September they were halted at the Rhine. At Arnhem in the Netherlands a combined airborne and ground forces operation composed of British, Canadian and Polish forces met unexpected German resistance. Their goal, to capture the various bridges over branches of the Rhine, completely failed, and many were trapped, taken prisoner and killed or injured. Royal Marine Commandos were involved in this, and my mother knew many of the casualties. The Allies were stuck for the moment.

Soon after the end of the war there was a British film "Theirs is the Glory" about Arnhem, part of it filmed during the operation. My mother wept as we watched it. And we felt her sorrow — not just for the Marines, but for the people of the Netherlands, who also suffered high casualties. And at my boarding school later on, the Royal School for Daughters of Officers of the Army, I met many girls who told me that their fathers had hated Field Marshall Mongomery, who had planned the Arnhem battle. "It was all his mistake" they said. Mistakes are too often made in war, but Montgomery was known for his arrogance.

So after that we just waited, through the 'doodlebug' attacks on the London area, through the battle of the Bulge, through the final invasion of Germany. But more and more I was occupied with my own thoughts and activities, and more pressures from outside. The war was always with us, but life in Exmouth was becoming increasingly interesting, as we all grew older and more of the local world was open to us.

I still loved drawing and painting, I took my sketchbooks with me everywhere and drew whatever appealed to me — rocks, flowers, landscapes, sometimes people or our cat Flippy. Friends and relatives' birthdays, Christmas, were preceded by a flurry of card production. I'd discovered a little shop downtown that had a stash of drawing and watercolor paper, which made things possible now that I'd used up all the end papers in my books. Its owner, old Mrs. Mair, helped me get some of my paintings framed.

And I read, if anything, more than ever — reading on beaches, busses, lying on the lawn on chilly summer days wrapped in a rug. My reading was shifting into grown up books — Daphne DuMaurier, John Buchan, Kipling's short stories, and some of the books on our bookshelves. That year my mother gave me for my birthday a grown up book called "Pilgrims of the Wild". It was by a man who was part Canadian Indian, and it told the story of his nurturing of a couple of orphaned beaver pups on the banks of Lake Huron. I loved it, still have it, and it gave me a picture of that lovely Ontario lake country that I recognized only twelve years later when Brian and I moved to Ontario with our children. And I continued to read the Ransome books as soon as they appeared. They were often donated by Georgie, who, despite nursing in a hospital in the midst of the V1 and V2 target area, managed to send us birthday and Christmas presents the same as ever. She was braver than we ever recognized at that time.

The 'Cormorant Club', with our competitions — for daring acts on the swing, climbing trees, high jumping and long jumping, as well as our continued battles against our 'enemies' on the street next door, went on as before. We learned semaphore in order to signal to each other from afar, taught by the drawings in the Arthur Ransome books. We were always hungry at this time — we were growing fast, and there was never quite enough at meals. We shook down the fruits from the decorative plum trees on the street and ate the nuts inside the pits. They tasted like almonds, we thought — but almost everything tasted good then.

Expeditions were longer, often down to the beaches by bike, and we started some new enterprises, among them the production of ointments to cure nettle stings. There were beds of nettle everywhere — difficult to avoid when following a stream to its source or exploring a bombed out building. One of our ointments was largely made of toothpaste stolen from the bathroom. Obviously we needed to test its efficacy on a victim of stinging nettles. So we found a large patch of particularly vicious looking plants, and sent Richard into it. He charged in without a word of protest, and emerged quite cheerfully, with a crop of red blisters arising on his arms and legs. We plastered him with our concoction, which he swore did the trick. Perhaps the toothpaste acted as a counter irritant. It seems unlikely that it really worked, but Richard still thinks so.

For me, it was a time when I finally learned to enjoy being with girls. They still, in order of precedence, came well below my gang, but there was a girl, Shirley Thompson, with whom I cycled to school, visited in her home, and did homework. There was another, Jane Shephard, another Marine daughter. She and I went to the same school too. My mother was friends with her mother, and Jane and I would try on dresses upstairs and once even ' borrowed' her mother's lipstick while the adults were drinking tea in the sitting room. We pranced downstairs to show them our finery, but my mother was horrified at the lipstick, and suspicious of Jane from then on. I was surprised that Jane's mother just seemed to find us amusing, but when our 'innocence' was threatened our mother's 'look' always appeared. The trouble was one could never tell what would provoke it!

A more approved friend was Doreen, known as 'Dorks' Aucott. She was an army daughter, but my mother liked her mother, and Dorks was a good blend of tomboy and sensible girl. She loved reading, was a better tree climber than I was, and had many more friends than I did, having lived in Exmouth longer. She now lived just round the corner. So gradually I found a circle of girls I liked, who invited me to their birthday parties and were friendly.

Among those girls, I only remember one father who was home. Apart from Betty Howard's father, 'Daddy Dear' as he was always known, they were all off in the armed forces, but I never again met anyone whose father was dead.'.

By the time 1945 began a shadow was beginning to loom over my future and that of many of the girls in Hythe House. We were all 'signed up' for various 'public' — really private, boarding schools, and these would be our last six months of being at home and going to local day schools.

I had been 'signed up' at birth — or close to it — for 'The Royal School' in Bath. The school had been founded in the mid 1800s for

Army officers' daughters, often sent home from the colonies to be educated when they reached ten or over. Of course many middle and upper class children were sent 'away' to school when they were much
younger, some as young as six. My mother, who had not gone to boarding school herself, thought this was a barbarous custom, but she also
recognized that going to the 'right' sort of school was very important in
Britain for social and career purposes — much more important to many
parents than whether it genuinely offered a superior education, or was
suited to the needs of their particular children.

I'm not sure what my mother thought of the Royal School, but it
qualified in the important respects, and my father had decided on it.
Also, it offered scholarships and graduated fees for children with financial needs. I was expected to get a scholarship. Luckily, the R.S., as we
always called it, turned out to be an excellent school, far ahead of its
time in many ways. But that was to be discovered later.

Meanwhile, my little school, Hythe House, geared itself up to make
sure I got the expected scholarship. There had never been anything
hard about school — I even sailed through math with no problems. But
Hythe House was really too easy. As I've said, most of the teachers
were previously housewives and mothers, often bright and interesting
women, but certainly not well prepared to push for academic achieve-
ment. I was thought of as 'clever'. So although I was well aware that I
needed to get that scholarship I had no idea of what it really entailed,
and the thought of it didn't worry me one bit. Perhaps if what I was
offered had been more challenging I might have worked harder, but I
went on getting glowing comments and top grades on my report cards
while most of my real learning came from my own reading and wasn't
included in the scholarship exam.

What did worry me, and what, of course, I could not tell my mother,
was that I was terrified of being sent off to live among a horde of girls.
Hythe House was relaxed and friendly — I had never been scared there
as I had been at Copplestone. But at day school one could escape at the
end of the day and cycle home to ones normal existence and freedom.
There was a certain excitement about the idea of boarding school, because the RS was still living in the place where it had been evacuated
from Bath at the beginning of the war. This was Longleat, the home of
the Marquess of Bath, a huge sixteenth century mansion in a vast park

in Wiltshire. The thought of Longleat almost overcame my fear, but not enough.

When another girl asked me if I was afraid the work at the RS would be too hard I replied, quite honestly for once, that I would just be afraid of the other girls. But it would have been no use to express that to my mother, or even to the Joyces. Joyce Kinge had been to the local state school, and had left at the regular school leaving age then, which was fourteen. Despite this, she was a reader, curious about everything, and learned quickly. Looking back, I'm surprised that she never told us more about her own childhood or schooling. I doubt if she was ashamed of it — Joyce was not ashamed of her background in any way, even in that class conscious society. But she may have been surprised and a bit envious that I was actually nervous about going to the R.S., when I was obviously so fortunate in most ways.

Joyce Hayter had been to boarding school herself, so accepted it as a necessity.

Going away to school was so normal, so inevitable, that it wasn't worth mentioning. My mother probably dreaded it as much as I did, but would never have shown it. Independent as I was in many ways, I too accepted my future schooling as inevitable, never really questioning its necessity.

But when I look back on it I learned a lot at Hythe House. There were things that have added more to my enjoyment of life than many of the requirements of my other schools ever did. It was a kind place, for one thing. Perhaps the lack of competition and the informality of the teachers prevented the sort of bullying and exclusion tactics that I'd encountered at Copplestone, and would later at the R.S. Sports, also, played a much less important role than they did at either school.

There was no gym, no auditorium, no science labs. In fact we barely had any science — just what used to be called "nature study". This consisted largely of botany, with the sex lives of flowering plants being as close as we ever got to studying human reproduction. Geography was interesting and fun — our teacher had traveled and we did a lot of map drawing and discussion mostly of European countries and the Empire and their ways of life. History was mostly British, and almost entirely political. In an area filled with ancient buildings and relics of the remote past we never looked at how people actually lived in the remote past. We learned Latin and French to a reasonable level. Even math. compared with what American children learn at eleven or twelve, was fairly advanced — but not by the standards of other, more conventional schools.

But — we had an inspiring art teacher, and an English teacher who loved poetry and plays and classics and modern novels. And we had a music teacher who taught us — all of us — to read music and to sing.

My 'form' (that meant class) would gather in what had been the drawing room of the house — the biggest room. There was a piano there, so it was also where we had our morning prayers, always with a hymn or two from the Church of England hymnal. They were the good hymns, with music from Handel, Holst, Purcell, Beethoven. In music class we sang old English folk songs — 'Annie Laurie' 'Cockles and Mussels', 'The Water is Wide'. We sang complicated arrangements of poems by Shakespeare, John Masefield, "The Shepherd's Song" by Elgar — and my favorite "Rolling down to Rio" with words by Rudyard Kipling and music by Edward German. We sang Christmas carols, and rounds, and learnt to use a few percussion instruments — triangles, cymbals, castanets. All of us sang — it was simply part of what our two elderly head mistresses considered a well rounded education.

Howard and Richard, at St. Peter's, sang some of the same songs, so that at home we would all sing together. I remember the boys tormenting me by singing Handel's "Where E're You Walk" and purposely repeating the first three lines without continuing — simply to annoy me. But I can still remember both words and music of all those songs.

We practiced the carols for our Nativity play, in which, to my trepidation, I was chosen to play the Virgin Mary. Wearing a long blue dress and a head scarf, my hair falling down my back, I nervously held a baby doll and sang, alone, a sentimental song called "We Will Rock Him". I felt stupid and out of my element — perhaps a bit of a fraud, having major doubts about Christianity. My mother commented that my voice didn't sound like me, and I could tell that she didn't mean that in any complimentary way. I was not a natural actor!

In English we all had anthologies of English poetry. We didn't just study one or two poems in detail. We would each choose one poem to learn and recite to the class. This led to browsing the whole book, and in my case finding so many I liked I had difficulty choosing. They varied in style and content. I found poems from every era that I read again and again — the Elizabethans, discovering that Sir Walter Raleigh was a poet as well as a courtier and adventurer; the first World War poets — Graves, Brooke, Sassoon; Wordsworth and Shelley and Coleridge, and the Victorians, Matthew Arnold and Tennyson and Hardy — even moving on to T.S. Eliot. Georgie gave me a book of poetry by Walter de la Mare which supplemented our school anthology. For my mother's birthday in 1944 I gave her a notebook in which I'd written many of my own favorites, with my own illustrations.

This all led to a love of poetry that I have kept to this day. I find so many people I know who say they dislike poetry, and I feel sorry for them, because it has given me so much pleasure. I'm sure that's because we had to choose from an excellent collection. Learning and reciting fixed it in our minds. There was little attempt to analyze, but the effect of finding what we liked led us to explore further, and interpret naturally as we grew older.

Our teacher, a mother of one of the girls, also read to us regularly. In this way we were exposed to books we might otherwise never have looked at. Some of them were popular fiction of the time. One was "The Pied Piper" by Neville Shute. This told the story of an elderly man who was trapped in France just before and during the Nazi invasion of 1940. He is entrusted with the care of two British children, and as he attempts to find a way back to Britain he is joined by several other children looking for refuge. It's an exciting, moving story, and had great appeal for me, feeding my obsession with the war.

I was already discovering how much history I was learning from the novels of Margaret Irwin — particularly "The Stranger Prince", a historical novel about Prince Rupert of the Rhine, a nephew of Charles I who became commander of the Royalist Cavalry in the English Civil War. It was a book that really drew you back into the seventeenth century, and I began to read all I could about the Civil war. So "The Pied Piper" made me realize I could find out about present day affairs by reading novels too.

And art — still one of my favorite occupations. Nothing specially different in the way of techniques, but much new knowledge of the art world. I knew about and recognized the work of many of the great artists of the past, through books and prints, though I'd still never gone to an art show or museum. But at Hythe House I discovered Picasso and Matisse. Both of them shocked, but also fascinated me. I experimentally tried to draw people in new ways, copying Picasso. My mother and Joyce, in turn, were shocked, and somewhat worried that I would change my realist approach.

I asked my grandfather Hayter what he thought of Picasso. "I hate 'im!" he replied sturdily. But though fascinated, and wanting to learn more, I was not entranced either. I preferred drawing people, and places, in the way I saw them.

So for me Hythe House was a success. But there were no national exams at that level, and no way for me or my mother to know that the Royal School might require something different in the way of preparation. So I did not get that scholarship. My mother was grumpy and disappointed, but I did get accepted at the school, and they did offer low fees for me, so all was not lost. And when I arrived at the RS I continued to get high grades, and not to work very hard.

But that was all ahead, and meanwhile the war, and my childhood, had to end.

Coming to the End

In the years since we came to Devon my mother had gradually recovered. She would never be the person she had been before the war — the years that ended with our time in Rochester. But she built up a life and a personality that might have looked the same to anyone who hadn't known her well before. Howard and I had, and we remembered. Perhaps Richard did too, though he had been very young when the war started.

She made friends, as she always had. We often went to the beach with the Pratts, and my mother and Mary Pratt gossiped and laughed together, as she always had done with friends. She found women she'd known slightly before — Marine wives, like her seeking safety from bombs, or having absent husbands based at the Lympstone training camp close by. As women often do, she met our friends' mothers, and liked some of them. She seemed to feel most at home with women who shared some part of her background.

I was excited for her when she was invited to go to a party at the Lympstone camp. It was probably some Marine anniversary or cere- mony — some formal occasion to which she was invited as an officer's widow — perhaps still officially a wife. I think she was excited too — it was a party, after all, and there hadn't been any of those for a long time. But she came home a little sad, and even managed to tell us — or did we overhear her telling Joyce or Mary Pratt? — that she had been as- signed to a young officer who had not known quite how to treat her. For once she felt awkward and unwelcome.

But generally it was obvious that men still fell for her. The few men still around — elderly neighbors, delivery men, our doctor — all paid her special attention. She flirted lightly with them, made friends with their wives, who never seemed to mind. But at no point did she ever appear to fall for anyone herself. Even when a distant cousin, a naval chaplain called Jack Wallace, came to visit and took her out one evening, the two of them departing arm in arm, we heard nothing more of him. Though the fact that she actually asked me if I liked him made me suspicious — I was terrified at the thought of her finding someone else and immediately said no. Perhaps she really did like him — perhaps I stopped her. I hope not. He seemed a nice man.

Sometimes, as when she had started to race us, she seemed to return to her previous fun loving self. She did the same at the boys' sports days at St. Peter's, where there was always a parents' race. Among all the other bare footed mothers she would be tearing along, usually winning, in her silk stockings and high heels. She would end up breathless and laughing, accepting amazed congratulations with a smile. Competition drew her out of herself — she enjoyed being a winner. Afterwards, at home, she'd retreat into her usual preoccupied self, cleaning, ironing, hard to approach.

But then again, sometimes she'd burst into a series of jokes or teasing, making us laugh so much that once on my way to the beach I wet my pants and had to put on my swim suit under my dress. On our picnics she would suddenly join us in a game of French cricket or rounders, played, very often, with makeshift bats picked up in fields or on beaches. She put up with endless days on the beach when it was cold and windy, just because we loved it so much. That was certainly a sign of love, even if we couldn't recognize it then. In cherry season, she still made earrings out of two sets of cherries, and pranced around with them hanging from her ears.

And on the rare occasions when we were really ill, like when I developed measles and my temperature was so high she could no longer ignore it, she actually called the doctor, made a fire in my bedroom fireplace, and played monopoly with us until my headache grew too bad. A fire was the ultimate luxury — I remember the comfort of the flickering flames reflected on the white walls as I drifted off to sleep. I could sit by the fire when she made my bed, and she brought my meals up to me.

Ordinary complaints, though, coughs and sneezes, aches and pains, even a badly sprained ankle that I incurred during one of our battles, received no sympathy at all, but were simply a nuisance. We were never allowed to stay home from school for even the worst cold. I guess this was fairly normal, because I don't think anyone ever complained about my runny nose or sneezes. It did mean that we were delighted to find that we had to be quarantined for chickenpox and measles. Heaven to stay home for at least two weeks!

Small sorrows, even big ones, as when my rabbit was killed, didn't seem to be considered important. They were most often simply ignored. But once, an event remembered because so rare, she noticed I was feeling miserable and asked "What's the matter, darling?" As it happened, my mood was really my own fault. We'd been out for a picnic in the country, and for once the Pratt boys and my brothers had refused to fall in with my plans. I was feeling forlorn and abandoned, but I'm sure their feelings were justified. I told her the problem. She listened quietly, then told me gently that sometimes I had to allow the boys to make their own plans. I felt warm and cared for.

I don't think any of us were in doubt that she loved us. What was missing was her enjoyment of us, which had existed certainly when we were babies and toddlers. Sarah was probably my mother's greatest comfort when my father died. Mum had always loved babies, and of course Sarah needed her attention more than we did. But perhaps, if she had allowed Sarah to be one of us instead of being always with her, I would not have felt so excluded.

We three older ones seemed to have become more of a responsibility than a pleasure for our mother. I used to wonder, as I grew older and increasingly aware of her underlying unhappiness, why she didn't find us a comfort. Back in 1945 we still needed comfort ourselves, even now the war was drawing to a close. We could, surely, have found comfort in each other and in her, if she had shown us how. But we hadn't been taught to look after each other — just scolded for fighting or arguing. She was still the most important person in our lives, and we wanted most of all to please her. We would have done anything for her, if she had ever declared a wish or a need, or expressed a feeling. But we were left searching, each of us left with our own fears and worries. We knew we had lost our father. Gradually, as we grew older, it seemed likely to me that we had, in a sense, lost our mother too. She was a victim of war, even if she had never been damaged physically.

I barely remember those last months of the war. More important were personal pleasures, like my first shorts — really culottes. Of course I had wanted shorts like my brothers' — boys' shorts with proper pockets, but that would have been too radical for my mother. To give way on any sort of trousers was a real concession from her. But I loved my shorts anyway, and stuffed their meager pockets with small tins of emergency supplies, left by the Yanks, and RAF silk maps, ceasing to be used by airmen, now that most of the continent was in Allied hands. We went further and further on our bikes. Sometimes the marines in the camp on Dalditch Common whistled at me, which made me uncomfortable. New workers, young men, began to be seen working on the roads. They were German prisoners, mostly friendly and cheerful, trying to make friends. They didn't look any different from anyone else. And the fear began to disappear.

Then one day it was the end. I can't remember the announcement, but I remember the joy. Perhaps it wasn't a beautiful day, but that was how it felt. Somehow, everyone found strings of flags, and every house was decorated. And the church bells rang, pealing out over the lovely countryside from every ancient church. We even went to church, and sang joyfully the familiar hymns of thanksgiving — "Now Thank We All our God, With Hearts and Hands and Voices, Who Wondrous Things Hath Done" and Blake's "Jerusalem" and "God Save the King". And we listened to the festivities in London, and speeches from the King and Winston Churchill. It was a glorious day.

A little while afterwards my mother called us all into her bedroom. She sat on the little curved stool by her dressing table and told us that our father was dead, that he had gone down with the Bonaventure in 1941. We were all silent. Then "I knew" I said. She seemed surprised. "How did you know?" she asked. I couldn't tell her. We quietly left her alone. We scattered, off to our various pursuits. None of us spoke to each other, and none of us ever asked her for more information.

It was too late for that.

EPILOGUE

That summer was much the same as any other, except that there was the shadow of boarding school looming over my head. Long days on the beach at Budleigh, lying on the rounded pebbles reading, diving into the waves into the clear, green-blue water, eating our familiar sandwiches and cold new potatoes — food was no easier to find and rationed even more severely. We were on the beach one glorious August day when someone came running to tell us the war in Asia was finally over. Oddly, considering my interest in such things, I do not remember a thing about the bombing of Hiroshima and Nagasaki. And for us, VJ Day was a bit of an anti climax. Our war had been over for three months.

We were actually able to go back to Portsmouth and see our grand-parents there. Going on the train was exciting, and we thought it would be good to see our old home again. It was fun to see Peter and Simon, but it was no longer 'home'.

Some time after that day my uncle Fred came back from the Japanese internment camp near Shanghai he'd been in since 1941. My mother didn't recognize him when he arrived one day, haggard, gray and very, very thin. His wife had died soon after the liberation, sick and worn out from all the deprivations they'd suffered.

And a little later, on the train to the Royal School for the scholar-ship exam, I began to learn about the Nazi concentration camps, and realize how easy our war had been.

So in September I left home for the first time, and began my new life at the Royal School. Childhood, the Cormorant Club, and my years of freedom were over. But the fear of war has never quite left me.

About Susan Mayall

Born in 1933 in England, Susan Mayall's memories of a wartime childhood in idyllic surroundings dominate her writing, despite an eventful life since: Cambridge University and meeting her husband - moves to Canada, Philadelphia and Livermore, California - raising four children, teaching history, founding and running Goodenough Books in Livermore - hiking, skiing, traveling, protesting wars. She has nine grandchildren, and two great grandchildren, and hopes all of them will read her book one day.

CPSIA information can be obtained
at www.ICGtesting.com
Printed in the USA
FSOW04n2305100917
38297FS

9 781595 946089